D0498256

THE WASHINGTON STATE HISTORICAL SOCIETY

In its 98th year
proudly joins in the commemoration of our state's

• CENTENNIAL ANNIVERSARY •

by offering this special edition of
WASHINGTON: IMAGES OF A STATE'S HERITAGE

• 1989 •

WASHINGTON

Images
of a
State's
Heritage™

WASHINGTON

Images
of a
State's
Heritage™

Carlos Schwantes • Katherine Morrissey • David Nicandri • Susan Strasser

*Sponsored by the
1989 Washington Centennial Commission
With generous support from
The Weyerhaeuser Company*

MELIOR PUBLICATIONS

Spokane, Washington

Melior Publications, P O Box 1905, Spokane, Washington 99210-1905.
Copyright © 1988 by Melior Publications. All rights reserved.
Images of a State's Heritage is a trademark of Melior Publications.
Printed in the United States of America.
The paper used in this publication meets the minimum
requirements of American National Standard for Information Science
permanence of paper for printed library materials, ANSI Z39.48, 1984.
95 94 93 92 91 90 89 88 10 9 8 7 6 5 4 3 2 1

Library of Congress Cataloging-in-Publication Data
Washington, images of a state's heritage.
    Includes index.
        1. Washington (State)—History—Pictorial works.
2. Washington (State)—Description and travel—
Views. I. Schwantes, Carlos A., 1945–
II. Washington Centennial Commission.
III. Weyerhaeuser Company.
F892.W35 1988 979.7'04 88-9488
ISBN 0-9616441-1-7

Table of Contents

Section III: The Modern Era 126

Foreword

Throughout our history Washington's character has been marked by diversity—diversity in people, lifestyles, and land forms. The variety found in Washington has added much to our lives. You will meet in the pages of *Washington* the Native Americans, immigrant settlers, and newcomers to Washington who have contributed so much to our state's culture. From George Bush, the first black settler in Washington Territory, and Mayor Bertha Landes of Seattle, to recent Mexican-American and Asian immigrants, *Washington* tells the stories of those who have shaped our history.

The first people on this land walked, paddled canoes, and rode horses. Now we cross the state by air in thirty-five minutes. Where once there were paths and dirt roads, now there are flashing rails and busy interstate freeways. Log cabins and tule mat lodges have gained skyscrapers as neighbors. *Washington* traces the growth and development of the state—the evolution of its boundaries, the controversies over the location of the new state's capital, the changes in the landscape created by Mount Saint Helens's fiery eruption, and much more.

We are surrounded and embraced by the beauty of Washington, by its rivers, deserts, forests, mountains, lakes, and ocean beaches. The land's abundant resources have been the basis for much of Washington's economic growth—timber, wheat, apples, fishing and canning, coal mining, and more. Our lives are shaped by the character of the land, and the Washington places so eloquently portrayed in these pages are at the heart of the experiences of Washingtonians.

The small events and forces as well as the large have their place in our history. The advent of the automobile, the apple craze that brought horticulturists to the state, the emergence of shopping centers in Washington, and the growth of suburbia are portrayed here along with the Great Depression, the world wars, and the building of Grand Coulee Dam. Each of us, every day, is making Washington State history. Some part of our history is captured in these pages—readers will be reminded of their own experiences by these images of our heritage.

We can indeed be proud of Washington State. Her people, shaped and strengthened by the events of the last one hundred years, are ready to face the challenges of the future with strength and vision. The 1989 Washington Centennial Commission, which we chair, has encouraged the publication of this book to bring the sweep of Washington's history into view. Knowledge of our past brings pride in our accomplishments and gives confidence to our efforts to build a strong and healthy Washington in our second century.

Jean Gardner
Ralph Munro
Co-Chairs, 1989 Washington Centennial Commission

A Sense of Place

What special qualities define the state of Washington? What gives its residents a sense of place distinct from that of California, Indiana, or Massachusetts? One simple and obvious answer is the state's environment, its spectacular natural setting: not just the stunning juxtaposition of mountains and water that characterizes the Olympic Peninsula and Columbia River Gorge, but also the vastness of its interior spaces filled with arid sagebrush plains and fertile rolling hills. Residents occasionally refer to their state as "God's Country," and the opening stanza of "America the Beautiful" could well describe its mountain ranges and amber waves of grain.

The number of slick coffee table books depicting the Washington landscape, the popularity of outdoor clothing and gear, downhill and cross-country skiing, boating, fishing, hunting, backpacking, camping, whitewater rafting, and a host of similar activities testify to a special relationship between Washington residents and their natural environment.

Indeed, in few other parts of the United States is the natural setting so intimately a part of a state's identity. Washington without its Cascade peaks, its rugged coastline, its Puget Sound fogs, its vast interior of sagebrush, rimrock, and big sky is as unthinkable as New England without a Puritan heritage, the South without the Lost Cause, the Midwest without its agricultural cornucopia, or California without its Gold Rush mentality.

Fundamental to a Washingtonian's sense of place is the awareness that much of the state remains uninhabited or only lightly populated. A person trapped in rush-hour traffic on one of Seattle's floating bridges may find that claim hard to believe. Yet the entire population of Washington, which in 1980 numbered 4.1

When Rufus Woods, publisher of the Wenatchee Daily World, *first proposed in 1918 to dam the Columbia River at the head of the Grand Coulee to provide water for irrigation and cheap electric power, skeptics abounded. Launched in 1934 and placed in service in 1941, the Grand Coulee Dam was called "The Eighth Wonder of the World." Its size dwarfed the army of workmen who found Depression-era jobs building the Grand Coulee Dam.* Courtesy of Minnesota Historical Society.

A Washington State ferry makes one of several daily dockings at Friday Harbor on San Juan Island, a picturesque town with restaurants, hotels, a fishing fleet, and a world class whale museum sponsored by the University of Washington. Courtesy of Washington State Tourism Division.

million—approximately equal to the population of Boston's metropolitan area—is spread out over sixty-eight thousand square miles, an expanse of land equal in size to the six New England states. Washington encompasses more land than England, Wales, and Northern Ireland combined.

To describe the population of Washington as spread out is technically correct but very misleading. Washingtonians tend to gather like bees into a few urban hives. More than half the population of Washington lives in a handful of counties that border the east side of Puget Sound and include the cities of Seattle, Tacoma, Everett, Bellingham, Bellevue, and Olympia.

Because Washingtonians cluster in urban areas, the population density of King County—the site of the Pacific Northwest's most populous city, Seattle—is 597 people per square mile. Still, some counties in eastern Washington have fewer than 6 people per square mile.

Even urban residents experience a strong sense of their natural setting. On days when the intermittent drizzle and leaden skies of winter clear, residents of Seattle and Tacoma draw fresh inspiration from the sight of Mount Rainier standing

Loggers, such as these near Grays Harbor, were responsible for Washington's status in 1910 as the leading producer of lumber, with 63 percent of its wageworkers employed in the forest products industry.
Courtesy of Washington State University Library.

majestically on the horizon. The Cascade Range likewise forms a backdrop for residents of Yakima, Ellensburg, and Wenatchee on the east side and is equally a part of their sense of place, while Spokane residents can enjoy a quiet lunch hour on the banks of the Spokane River in the middle of downtown.

The composite city stretching from Everett to Olympia—sometimes referred to as Pugetopolis—is ninety miles long but narrow enough to afford boaters and fishermen easy access to the open waters of Puget Sound in one direction, and backpackers, skiers, and hunters convenient escape to the Cascade Range in the other. It is only an hour's drive from the shores of Puget Sound to the ski slopes at Snoqualmie Pass.

The landforms of Washington are not merely matters of geology and real estate, but also of aesthetics and culture. The most recurrent theme in Washington literature is the interaction of people with their natural environment. Landforms also serve as the backdrop against which much of the state's history is played out.

Mountains contribute to the marked irregularity of natural and human landscapes in Washington. Unlike the prairie states, where rectangular fields of corn, soybeans, and wheat extend to the horizon, many parts of Washington appear rugged and unfinished. Except for state and international boundaries and some city streets, straight lines are not common features of the Washington landscape. The coastline is very irregular and land uplifted into sinuous hills gives the Palouse country in July and August the appearance of a swelling ocean of wheat. To become visually accustomed to the Washington landscape is crucial to developing a sense of place.

Almost every place-name on the map of Washington has a story behind it. Some are biographical, some capsule histories. Names that recall the region's first residents identify physical features such as Snoqualmie Pass and Moses Lake, and such localities as the counties of Snohomish, Skagit, Yakima, Spokane, and Walla Walla. The names Puget Sound, Mounts Rainier and Saint Helens, the

Raking sage to clear Kittitas County for crops in 1929. Courtesy of National Archives.

Strait of Juan de Fuca, the San Juan Islands, and the Columbia River remind us of still another aspect of Washington's history: the era of the North Pacific maritime frontier. Still more names— Clarkston, Lewis County, Clark County, Fort Lewis—testify to the importance of Meriwether Lewis and William Clark, the two explorers who have long symbolized the westering impulse in American life.

Like the names that are a part of every Washingtonian's sense of place, the paintings and photographs on the pages that follow are capsule histories. Each illustrated essay seeks to capture an important facet of Washington's heritage. Naturally, concrete subjects are easier to illustrate than abstract or complex issues such as the "money question" that agitated Washington politics a century ago. We left such questions to the standard history texts.

The authors have taken pains to select only quality images. Washington is fortunate to have had photographers and artists like Asahel Curtis, Clark and Darius Kinsey, Frank Matsura, Charles Pratsch, Frank Palmer, Gustavus Sohon, and others capture its heritage.

This book is a collaborative effort in every sense of the word. Thus we do not identify the authors of individual essays. In addition to the names listed on the title page we were fortunate to be able to call upon the talents of John Shideler, Hal Rothman, Barbara Chamberlain, and

Chrystle Snider of Futurepast: The History Company, Melior Publications' corporate parent.

Others to whom we are indebted are Larry Workman, Quinault Indian Nation tribal forester; Kathryn Hinsch, Microsoft; Vivian Adams and Agnes Tulee, Yakima Nation Museum; Louis Flannery and Susan Seyl, Oregon Historical Society; Gene Tollefson, Bonneville Power Administration; Drew Crooks, Washington State Capital Museum; Frank Green, Joy Werlink, Richard Frederick, and Marie DeLong, Washington State Historical Society; Carolyn Margolis, Pete Daniel, and Rebecca Zurier, Smithsonian Institution; Helen Kilgour, Royal Ontario Museum; Carla Rickerson, Suzzallo Library, University of Washington; Linda Ziemer, Chicago Historical Society; Marilynn Phipps, Boeing Archives; Danielle Gerard, Boeing Commercial Airplane Company; Simon Siegl, Washington Wine Institute; William Taylor and Thomas Stilz, Washington State Tourism Bureau; Judy Gish, Port of Tacoma; Frances Hare, Yakima Valley Museum; Laura Bowler, Stark Museum of Art, Orange, Texas; K. L. Croskey, Naval Historical Foundation; Beth Carroll-Horrocks, American Philosophical Society; Carolyn Marr and Howard Giske, Museum of History and Industry; Edward Nolan, Eastern Washington State Historical Society; Joan Dutcher, National Maritime Museum, San Francisco; and George Miles, Beinecke Rare Book and Manuscript Library, Yale University.

Special thanks go to the Institute for Pacific Northwest Studies at the University of Idaho.

Melior Publications extends a special thanks to Elaine Miller, Washington State Historical Society; Richard Engeman, Suzzallo Library, University of Washington; and Doug Olson, Eastern Washington State Historical Society, for their patience and hard work in processing numerous photograph orders.

Melior Publications expresses its deep appreciation to the 1989 Washington Centennial Commission for its sponsorship and partial funding under contract of this project. In particular we are grateful to Jean Gardner and Ralph Munro, co-chairs of the commission, to Wilfred R. Woods, vice-chair, and to the chair of the publications committee, Dr. David Stratton, for their support and encouragement.

We are also pleased to recognize the other members of the publications committee: vice-chair Charlotte Paul, Barry Anderson, Barbara Dolliver, John Fahey, Ruth Kirk, Barbara Krohn, Dr. Alex McGregor, Julie Neff, Barry Provorse, Dr. Robert Skotheim, William Stimson, and Elizabeth Yee.

For their assistance and cooperation we also thank Putnam Barber, executive secretary, and staff members Jane McCurdy and Maura Craig.

Melior Publications expresses special gratitude to the Weyerhaeuser Company, which contributed paper for this book. In particular we thank George H. Weyerhaeuser, president; W. H. Meadowcroft, assistant to the president; and Robert F. Meyer, vice president–paper, Weyerhaeuser Paper Company, for their generous assistance.

Bathers at Liberty Lake, a popular resort located east of Spokane. From the early twentieth century until the automobile era of the 1920s, vacationers reached the lake by electric interurban trains. The railroad company maintained a dance and dining pavilion and floating pier. Courtesy of Eastern Washington State Historical Society.

I: The First Washingtonians

Canoe Columbia Riv

This sketch, entitled *"Canoe, Columbia River,"* shows presumably Chinook Indians plying the waterway, perhaps having adapted European sailing techniques to their indigenous craft. The drawing has been attributed to Edward Belcher, who explored the Northwest coast during the late 1830s. Courtesy of Special Collections Division, University of British Columbia.

More than anything else, it was geographical isolation that shaped the course of Washington's early history. Far longer than most temperate areas of the world, the North Pacific Coast remained beyond the reach of Europe and the rest of America. The region's geographical isolation in turn contributed to a pronounced lag in its historical developments. The frontier seemed to linger longer, and social and economic changes that evolved over a period of decades elsewhere were telescoped into a much briefer period of time in Washington, or skipped entirely.

The year 1776 offers a good promontory from which to observe Washington's chronological isolation. In Philadelphia, thirteen American colonies formally declared their independence from Great Britain on July 4 and set forth on an uncharted political course. Only eight days later the distinguished explorer Captain James Cook sailed from Plymouth, England, on his third great voyage of discovery. That venture, which neatly coincided with the course of the American Revolution, had important consequences for the Pacific Northwest. It signaled the region's emergence as a resource-rich area open to exploitation by more developed parts of the world.

Cook's ships reached the coast of Oregon in early 1778, then sailed north past future Washington to Nootka Sound on Vancouver Island. During the month that Cook's expedition remained at Nootka to repair its ships, crew members exchanged trinkets with the Indians for luxuriant sea otter pelts, some of which they used for shipboard bedding. These pelts—acquired in a most casual fashion—later proved to be a surprisingly valuable treasure. Cook was killed in the Hawaiian Islands, but as the survivors headed for home along the coast of China

they discovered that sea otter pelts from Nootka Sound were worth a fortune in Canton. The desire to return for more pelts nearly brought the crew to mutiny, but the officers prevailed and the two ships sailed for England.

Publication of the expedition's official records in 1784 gave the Pacific Northwest a clearly defined place in European imperial and commercial systems for the first time. But even before that date, news about the expedition had set in motion a commercial rush to exploit the fur resources of the Northwest coast.

Cook's voyage ended the previous pattern of sporadic and haphazard European contact with the Pacific Northwest and its native peoples. As an increasing number of fur traders from several nations cruised its coastal waters, it became obvious that a new era had dawned for the Northwest's first inhabitants: the Indians.

At Nootka Sound, Cook's crew members made extensive contact with the area's natives. Despite the fact that each culture found aspects of the other strange, there was no indication that the Nootka regarded Europeans as superior to or more powerful than themselves. At that time neither group dominated the other; their trading relations were for the most part friendly. Cook's voyage thus represented a harbinger of more extensive contacts to come, not an end to the Indian way of life.

The Indians of Nootka Sound were only one of many groups that resided in what anthropologists classify as the Northwest Coast cultural area. A separate area that existed east of the Cascade Range is known as the Plateau cultural area. Within the two areas were a variety of subgroups commonly called tribes.

Indians of the Northwest Coast cultural area occupied a narrow fringe of North American territory extending from

The Makah, who lived on the northernmost tip of the Olympic Peninsula, were famed for their skill as whalers. Photograph by Asahel Curtis courtesy of Special Collections Division, University of Washington Libraries.

southern Alaska to northern California. Mild climate, heavy rainfall, lush forests, an abundance of food and leisure time, a rich and varied material culture, and home sites on sheltered bays and harbors characterized their habitat. The people of the Coast cultural area developed a common dependence upon marine resources, canoe navigation, and a material culture that emphasized woodworking. They were among the finest woodworkers in the world.

Despite their common characteristics, Indians of the Coast cultural area were divided from one another by the rugged land and the barriers posed by language and locally oriented forms of society and government. Their primary social and

political unit was the extended family, represented in certain tribes beginning in the nineteenth century by free-standing totem poles—essentially family crests.

Like the Indians of the Coast area, those of the Plateau cultural area formed numerous tribes, bands, and families. Depending upon the season, the Plateau people engaged in various types of food gathering and preserving activities. The major rivers of the interior provided them with a diet rich in salmon. They dried fish and ground a nutritious fish meal for later use and for trade. They dug several kinds of roots such as wild turnip and the starchy bulb of the camas. They also harvested berries in season and hunted deer and other game. Some Plateau

Spectacular "Peluse Falls," depicted in a lithograph John Mix Stanley prepared for the Pacific Railroad Survey of the 1850s. The area is now a state park. Courtesy of Special Collections Division, University of Washington Libraries.

peoples even hunted bison, which appear to have lived on the Columbia Plateau in limited numbers until the 1770s.

The main meeting place for the peoples of the Coast and the Plateau was at the Dalles of the Columbia River. Here was the cosmopolitan center of Northwest Indian life, site of great month-long trade fairs analogous to those held in medieval Europe, a time for trading, dancing, ceremonial displays, games, gambling, and even marriages. Sometimes several thousand Indians came to trade salmon meal and bison robes from the interior for marine shells and beads, canoes, and fish oil from the coast. Those trade goods have been found as far away as Alaska, southern California, and Missouri.

The commerce in furs that began in the 1780s contributed greatly to European and American knowledge of the far Northwest but had a disruptive influence on Indian cultures. Traders and explorers from Europe and the United States brought diseases to which the Indians had no immunity. Smallpox, malaria, measles, and influenza—all were deadly killers. Disease wiped out whole villages on the lower Columbia River between 1829 and 1833 and quickly reduced some tribes to one-tenth their former size. By the time missionaries and settlers came to the Oregon Country in the 1830s, the region's Indian population was but a fraction of what it had been.

Motivating the explorers and traders from Russia, Spain, Great Britain, France, and the United States were the three Cs of empire: *curiosity, conquest,* and *commerce.* Rarely were those three forces separate from one another. Twenty-seven years after James Cook sailed along the Northwest coast, an overland expedition led by Lewis and Clark reached the mouth of the Columbia River in late 1805. Although the two ventures differed in

obvious ways, they had certain common features: both were military expeditions, both sketched in blank spots on the map of North America, and both spurred the commerce in furs. Publication of both the official and unofficial records of each expedition stimulated the curiosity and commercial ambition of those who followed.

Joining forces with curiosity, conquest, and commerce was competition. President Thomas Jefferson sent Lewis and Clark west in response to the competitive threat of British and Canadian fur companies. Reports from Lewis and Clark in turn spurred competitors from the north. Yet by the early 1820s the Hudson's Bay Company was the only fur enterprise of significance that still operated in the Pacific Northwest. No enterprise had a greater impact on Washington's early history than this British fur company.

The Hudson's Bay Company formed an empire that stretched from the Atlantic to the Pacific Ocean and north to the Arctic. Hundreds of establishments, with thousands of employees, were spread over millions of square miles. Head of the company's vast Columbia Department from 1824 to 1846 was Dr. John McLoughlin. From his headquarters at Fort Vancouver, and through a series of subordinate forts, he presided over a territory far larger than Great Britain itself.

McLoughlin and the Hudson's Bay Company maintained an extraordinary presence in a remote, frontier region. Fort Vancouver constituted a small, almost self-sufficient community that included a hospital, thirty to fifty small houses where employees lived with their Indian wives, and storehouses for furs, trading goods, and grain. There were also workshops where blacksmithing, carpentry, barrel making, and other activities were carried out. Here were located Washington's first sawmill, shipyard, gristmill, dairy, orchard, and library.

During the years the Hudson's Bay Company dominated the Oregon Country, United States citizens retained free access to the region under treaties negotiated with Great Britain. But few Americans moved to the far Northwest until encouraged by missionary activity in the late 1830s. Marcus and Narcissa Whitman established a mission among the natives of the Walla Walla Valley in 1836, but ironically they and other missionaries were far less successful in converting Indians to Christianity than in helping to encourage further white migration to the

"Old Fort Walla Walla," a Hudson's Bay Company post at the confluence of the Columbia and Walla Walla rivers. As Fort Nez Perce, it served as a trade and supply center for the Snake River country. Courtesy of Washington State University Library.

During the last two decades of the eighteenth century, Nootka Sound on the west coast of Vancouver Island was a busy place as European and American trading ships made ports of call seeking furs from the Indians as part of a global trading system. Courtesy of Special Collections Division, University of Washington Libraries.

Pacific Northwest.

Aiding would-be migrants from the Midwest was the opening of the Oregon Trail in the early 1840s. Stretching two thousand miles from the Missouri Valley to the Willamette Valley, the trail enabled hundreds, then thousands of pioneer families to make the six-month journey to the new Northwest.

The 1840s recorded some of the most momentous changes in Pacific Northwest history. When the decade dawned the Oregon Country had no political boundaries and no effective government apart from the influence of Hudson's Bay Company officials and American missionaries. Ten years later an international boundary divided the country along the forty-ninth parallel, and the Hudson's Bay Company had shifted its main operation to the British side of the border. Thousands of land-hungry settlers replaced fur traders and missionaries as typical white inhabitants. In the Willamette Valley, where most people settled, they laid out farms, towns, and roads. They organized a government for themselves in 1843, and five years later pressured Congress into creating the Oregon Territory. Finally, in a change that

no one wanted, the Whitman Massacre of 1847 marked the beginning of three decades of periodic warfare between Indians and settlers.

The Oregon Territory encompassed an enormous geographical area—approximately 350,000 square miles—that was never truly unified. People living in the scattered settlements north of the Columbia River, in what was then termed Northern Oregon, believed that Willamette Valley farmers dominated territorial affairs and neglected the interests of others. Settlers meeting at Cowlitz Prairie in August 1851 and at Monticello (now Longview) in November 1852 petitioned Congress to grant them a separate territory. The government responded in 1853 by creating a sprawling new territory named for George

Washington. Few other American territories were launched with so small a population, numbering fewer than four thousand non-Indian residents.

The territory's first governor was Isaac I. Stevens, a young Massachusetts native and officer in the Corps of Engineers. A man of abundant energy, he combined the roles of governor, Indian agent, and chief of a national railroad survey to further his dream of building a new society in the Pacific Northwest.

Stevens concluded a series of treaty negotiations with the Indians of Washington Territory, which then included Montana and northern Idaho, in which they relinquished title to more than sixty-four million acres of land in exchange for the retention of fishing rights and various federal allowances or annuities and instructions and tools for farming. Native Americans greatly resented the results of the treaty making, and warfare erupted on both sides of the Cascade Range. Some treaty provisions dealing with Indian fishing rights were still contested more than a century later.

Until the completion of a northern transcontinental railroad in 1883, Washington and the Pacific Northwest remained one of the most isolated areas of the United States, both in a physical and historical sense. Sentiments arising from the American Revolution were little more

Though their reservation is now located in the state of Idaho, the Nez Perce once ranged over wide portions of the future states of Oregon and Washington. Shown here is a painting of a "Nezperee" done by Canadian artist Paul Kane. Courtesy of Royal Ontario Museum, Toronto.

than political heirlooms brought by settlers from other parts of the United States. The Civil War, too, had only an indirect impact on the nation's far corner.

Probably well past the era of the actual Oregon Trail, these ladies stand beside an itinerant wagon that could have been their own. Courtesy of Washington State Historical Society.

Portraits of Native American Life

The myth of the "vanishing Indian" was an article of faith for white Americans in the nineteenth century. They believed that as the cultural and economic influence of the United States spread, the native peoples of the West were doomed to extinction. That myth influenced government policy toward Indians and became a stock item in American literature and oratory.

Some of the greatest popularizers of the myth were artists who traveled across the West for the purpose of preserving Indians on canvas before they vanished. Those artists were uniformly sympathetic to the plight of their subjects. Their paintings circulated from city to city in the East and were frequently marketed to potential viewers as the last chance to see a part of aboriginal America before it disappeared.

One of the first, and certainly the best-known of the self-appointed chroniclers of Native American life, was George Catlin. During the 1830s Catlin traveled up the Missouri River to paint the tribes living along its banks. When Catlin brought his canvases back to the "states" and later to Europe, he created a sensation. Catlin spent only a brief time in the far Northwest, so other artists assumed responsibility for documenting the Indians of the Oregon Country.

Canadian Paul Kane visited the Oregon Country with personnel from the

Paul Kane's eye for the material trappings of native life is shown in this sketch of Clallam traveling lodges. Courtesy of Stark Museum of Art, Orange, Texas.

Like virtually every ethnographer to visit the Northwest Coast, Kane was fascinated by the native use of masks. Courtesy of Stark Museum of Art, Orange, Texas.

the Pacific Northwest's own Edward S. Curtis. He used his camera to record the look of native life near the turn of the twentieth century, and even borrowed a page from Stanley's book by entitling one of his photographs "The Last of Their Race."

Prized though their artistry might be, Catlin, Curtis, Kane and others were very wrong. The native people of Washington and elsewhere survived disease and deceit. Their cultural identities have been preserved. Indians today have a political strength that would have been unimaginable a century ago.

Hudson's Bay Company in 1846–48. His work created the most comprehensive visual archive of the Northwest's native peoples at a time of early contact with the encroaching culture of white Americans. People today might decry the circumstances that inspired a collection like Kane's, yet students of native cultures have been greatly aided by its ethnographic content—dress, hairstyle, and body decoration. Kane's work, like that of Catlin, John Mix Stanley, and others, forms a priceless documentary record of an era.

After the artists came photographers to perpetuate the myth of the "vanishing American." The best known of those was

"Drying Piahe—Yakima" by Edward S. Curtis, shows a woman preparing "Pi-yaxi," or the bitterroot (a staple in the diet of Columbia Plateau people). Courtesy of Washington State Historical Society.

Empires By Land and Sea

Although most Pacific Northwesterners today speak English, it could have been otherwise. If revolutionary turmoil in France had not weakened the Spanish monarchy, the whole course of North American history might have been different.

Anglocentrism often causes Northwesterners to slight Hispanic contributions to the region's history. This is particularly unfortunate because the claim of the United States to the Columbia River country was based in part on Spanish claims transferred to the United States in the Adams-Onís Treaty of 1819. Spaniards also were the first Europeans to establish a colony in the future state of Washington when Salvador Fidalgo launched a short-lived agricultural outpost at Neah Bay on May 29, 1792.

The accomplishments of the British navigator, Captain James Cook, quickened the pace of exploration during the last quarter of the eighteenth century. Because of Cook, Spain intensified Pacific Basin exploration and showed renewed interest in locating the Northwest Passage. Bruno de Hezeta detected but did not sight or cross the bar of the Columbia River, a waterway later named for the ship of the Yankee fur trader Robert Gray, who rediscovered the Columbia in 1792.

The grandest Spanish exploring party was headed by Alejandro Malaspina, who arrived on the Northwest coast in 1791. His was the quintessential voyage of the Enlightenment era. Malaspina explored coastlines, cataloged new flora and fauna, and made ethnological observations.

The mission of Captain George Vancouver in 1792 was twofold—to exact territorial concessions agreed upon in Europe from his Spanish counterpart,

Images of the Washington Cascades, such as this one of Mt. Rainier, first appeared in print with the publication of George Vancouver's journal. This initial view of Washington's most prominent landmark appeared as a steel engraving of a sketch by John Sykes. Courtesy of Special Collections Division, University of Washington Libraries.

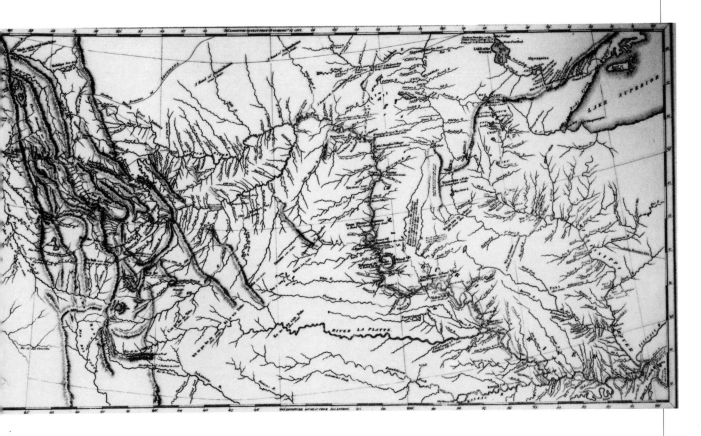

The Corps of Discovery's cartography was one of the primary contributions of William Clark. His field maps, when combined into this composite view, provided the first reasonably accurate assessment of the continent's width and the placement of the major mountain chains and river systems of the Northwest. Courtesy of American Philosophical Society, Philadelphia.

Bodega y Quadra, and to conduct the definitive search for the Northwest Passage. Vancouver's diplomatic mission was inconclusive, but his expedition explored Puget Sound, which he named for one of his lieutenants, Peter Puget.

At the turn of the nineteenth century, Europeans and Americans knew more about the islands of the Pacific Ocean than about the western half of North America. Alexander Mackenzie, a Canadian fur trader, led the first party of whites across the continent, reaching the coast of future British Columbia in 1793. Mackenzie's journal, published in 1801, was a masterpiece of discovery literature.

Spurred by the discoveries of Mackenzie and Gray, and concerned over Spanish consolidation of its claims north of Mexico, President Thomas Jefferson conceived the idea of an American Corps

of Discovery that would strengthen America's continental reach. The result was the scientific expedition of Meriwether Lewis and William Clark.

President Jefferson provided the corps with specific instructions to study geography, ethnography (native customs, alliances, and trade possibilities), and nature in the Northwest—its geology, weather, agricultural prospects, and animal and plant life.

The Lewis and Clark exploration of the Missouri and Columbia rivers during 1804–06 opened up the Rocky Mountain country to the fur trade and established a crude Northwest trade passage across the Continental Divide. The maps and sketches that resulted from the Lewis and Clark expedition provided a graphic portrayal of the continent's width and principal features.

The Beaver Trade

One immediate result of the Lewis and Clark expedition was the overland fur trade. John Jacob Astor organized the Pacific Fur Company in 1810 with plans in mind for a grand triangular trade between New York, the Pacific Northwest, and the Orient. Astor's enterprise never proved profitable and his agents sold their Oregon Country assets to a rival Canadian firm, the North West Company of Montreal, during the War of 1812.

The two most lasting legacies of the Astor experiment were the settlement at the mouth of the Columbia River that bears his name, and the almost accidental discovery of a route to the far Northwest that later would be immortalized as the Oregon Trail.

The Nor'westers of Canada faced the same problems that confronted Astor's men. The Columbia River watershed was never the fur district that had been

Fort Vancouver, the main British outpost in the Oregon Country, is shown in this lithograph based upon a sketch drawn by H. J. Warre and first published in 1848. Courtesy of Public Archives of Canada, Ottawa.

predicted. The beavers were fewer in number and their pelts less luxuriant because the winters were more temperate there than in the Rocky Mountains. Nor did native peoples serve as willing partners in the trade. The Indians of the Oregon Country were relatively affluent, and that diminished the allure of Euro-American trade goods.

In 1821 the Hudson's Bay Company absorbed the Nor'westers in a merger arranged in England. A former Nor'wester, Dr. John McLoughlin, headed the company's sprawling Columbia District. His base of operations was Fort Vancouver, established in 1825.

That fort, now located in Vancouver,

Washington, served as the gateway to a host of trading posts that dotted the Inland Northwest and included Forts Colville, Okanogan, and Walla Walla. In an early day attempt at corporate diversification, McLoughlin encouraged the formation of subsidiaries that would produce lumber and food for export to the Russian and Spanish colonies on the

Pacific Coast. Fort Nisqually (1833) began as one of those corporate farms.

The tide of American emigration to the Oregon Country in the 1840s contributed to the demise of Hudson's Bay Company fortunes. The growing settlements of British-hating Yankees, the inevitable decline of the fur trade, the dangerous Columbia River bar, and general uncertainty over the eventual boundary between Canada and the United States, caused the Hudson's Bay Company to move its regional headquarters to Fort Victoria on Vancouver Island in the late 1840s. The often romanticized fur trade era ended with the spread of the more mundane agricultural frontier.

The early Western artist Alfred Jacob Miller made the fur traders and trappers his specialty. In this watercolor painting, entitled "Trapping Beaver," Miller shows two mountain men at work. Courtesy of Walters Art Gallery, Baltimore.

The Americanization of Oregon

The westward movement of pioneer settlers was a central feature of American life in the nineteenth century. The advance guard of Euro-American settlement in the Oregon Country was Protestant missionaries who sought to evangelize the region's native peoples. Marcus and Narcissa Whitman established a mission in the Walla Walla Valley in 1836. But the cultural gulf between the well-intentioned evangelists and their supposed flock was immense and never successfully bridged, as the killing of the Whitmans in 1847 proved.

Indeed, it was their almost total failure to convert the Cayuse and Walla Walla peoples that led the Whitmans and other Protestant missionaries to spend much of their time recruiting settlers. Immigrants, they believed, would aid the economic development of their stations, make missionary work easier, and provide the Indians with role models for civilized life. The tactic actually had the opposite effect, because native peoples feared that white settlers would displace them.

Missionaries contributed to a wave of promotional literature that extolled the benefits of the Oregon Country. When combined with the efforts of secular promoters such as Hall Jackson Kelley and Nathaniel Wyeth, they inspired such a flood of American emigration to the far Northwest that a native leader is reputed to have urged his people to move east because apparently that country was becoming vacant.

At one time, American Fourth of July orators ascribed essentially political motives to the Oregon settlers by claiming that they went west to thwart Great Britain and save the Oregon Country for the United States. One historian wrote

A few early artists traveled the Oregon Trail. This view of the epic road west was probably prepared by George Gibbs, who went overland to Fort Vancouver with the army in 1849. It originally appeared in a government report on that expedition.
Courtesy of Washington State Historical Society.

that surely "something of formidable proportions must have sustained men who dared take their families on a 2,000 mile journey described in some newspapers as 'palpable homicide' without even assurance in the earliest period, that the emigrants of the preceding year had been successful."

A reading of pioneer diaries and letters now makes it clear that concern for physical health outranked politics as an inducement to migration. Diseases such as measles, mumps, cholera, smallpox, and dysentery regularly took a toll of American lives in the nineteenth century. In the 1840s, the greatest killers in the Mississippi Valley—the source of most westward migration—were malaria and tuberculosis.

As a result of epidemics, entire communities were frequently abandoned. Reports of the Oregon Country's free and rich lands, great rivers and forests, and mild and healthful climate as described by the Whitmans and others lured settlers to the Pacific Northwest.

The Oregon Trail has taken on mythic qualities in our regional and national history. One of the more enduring images is that of wagon trains heading west in single file, as if emigrants were driving along a narrow highway. They did wear ruts in the soft sandstone crossing the narrow defiles in the vicinity of the Continental Divide. But oxen and horses needed grass, and if someone's stock had gone before and eaten all the forage, an overlander had to leave the beaten path. The search for water, game, or wood for campfires, to say nothing of a desire to avoid the dust of the wagon in front, often forced drivers to swing wide of the main trail. At some points, the Oregon "Trail" was actually forty miles wide.

In the years before 1840 a vanguard of fur traders and missionaries established

Overland Emigration to Oregon Country			
1840	13	1850	6,000
1841	24	1851	3,600
1842	125	1852	10,000
1843	875	1853	7,500
1844	1,475	1854	6,000
1845	2,500	1855	500
1846	1,200	1856	1,000
1847	4,000	1857	1,500
1848	1,300	1858	1,500
1849	450	1859	2,000
		1860	1,500

From John D. Unruh, *The Plains Across* (University of Illinois Press).

the routes and posts that would later guide and sustain overland parties. Beginning in the early 1840s, the number of American settlers who moved to Oregon increased from a dozen a year to several thousand. Their growing numbers shifted the balance of power in the far Northwest between the United States and Great Britain, and between settlers and native peoples.

A common but erroneous impression is that Indians attacked and killed thousands of Oregon-bound pioneers. In fact, the major threat to overland travelers was Indian theft, typically of horses, not physical harm. No emigrants were killed during the early years of the movement (1840–44). This fact encouraged larger parties of settlers to venture forth, and joining them after 1849 was a boisterous crowd of gold seekers bound for California. The growing traffic and the arrival of white brigands caused trouble along the trail in the 1850s.

Overlanders killed more Indians than vice versa. Also, contrary to their reputation in the popular media, the Sioux and Pawnee Indians were not primarily responsible for the emigrant deaths that did occur. Ninety percent of the pioneers who died as a result of Indian attack were west of South Pass

The wreck of the Peacock *on the bar of the Columbia, as drawn by Alfred T. Agate.* Courtesy of Naval Historical Foundation and Smithsonian Institution.

The Whitman Mission at Waiilatpu near present Walla Walla. The watercolor by William Henry Jackson is based on survivors' recollections. Courtesy of National Park Service.

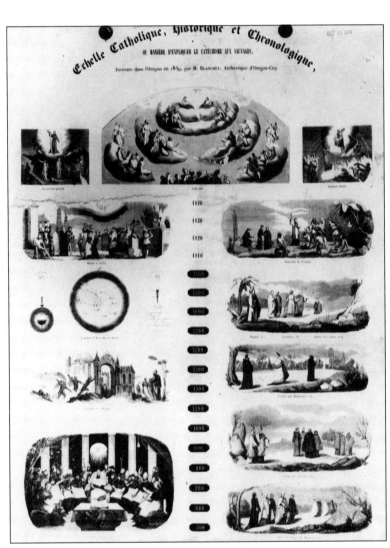

Another of the notable facets of the missionary era was a virulent sectarian strife. The weapons in this "cold war" between Catholic and Protestant missionaries were their respective "ladders" that were intended as graphic instructional devices for the Indians. These instruments said as much, if not more, about the supposed character faults of the competition as they did Christian salvation. Shown here is a section of the Catholic Ladder, picturing church history from the year 500 to 1840. Courtesy of Oregon Historical Society.

This Protestant Ladder was prepared in response to the Catholic Ladder by the Reverend H. H. and Eliza Spalding, circa 1845. Courtesy of Oregon Historical Society.

Emigrants Killed by Indians; Indians Killed by Emigrants		
	Emigrants	Indians
1840	0	0
1841	0	1
1842	0	0
1843	0	0
1844	0	0
1845	4	1
1846	4	20
1847	24	2
1848	2	2
1849	33	60
1850	48	76
1851	60	70
1852	45	70
1853	7	9
1854	35	40
1855	6	10
1856	20	15
1857	17	30
1858	?	?
1859	32	10
1860	25	10
Total	362	426

From John D. Unruh, *The Plains Across* (University of Illinois Press).

CIRCULAR.

TO THE OREGON EMIGRANTS.

GENTLEMEN:

It being made my duty, as Superintendent of Indian affairs, by an Act passed by the Legislature of Oregon, "to give such instructions and directions to Emigrants to this Territory, in regard to their conduct towards the natives, by the observance of which, they will be most likely to maintain and promote peace and friendship between them and the Indian tribes through which they may pass," allow me to say in the first place, that the Indians on the old road to this country, are friendly to the whites. They should be treated with kindness on all occasions. As Indians are inclined to steal, keep them out of your camps. If one or two are admitted, watch them closely. Notwithstanding the Indians are friendly, it is best to keep in good sized companies while passing through their country. Small parties of two or three are sometimes stripped of their property while on their way to this Territory, perhaps because a preceding party promised to pay the Indians for something had of them, and failed to fulfil their promise. This will show you the necessity of keeping your word with them in all cases.

There is another subject upon which I would say a few words. A number of the emigrants of 1845 took a cut off, as it is called, to shorten the route, leaving the old road; the consequence was, they were later getting in, lost their property, and many lost their lives. Some of those who reached the settlements, were so broken down by sickness, that it was some months before they recovered sufficient strength to labor.

A portion of the emigrants of 1846 took a new route, called the southern route. This proved very disastrous to all those who took it. Some of the emigrants that kept on the old road, reached this place as early as the 13th of September, with their wagons, and all got in, in good season, with their wagons and property, I believe, except a few of the last party. While those that took the southern route, were very late in reaching the settlements—they all lost more or less of their property—many of them losing all they had and barely getting in with their lives; a few families were obliged to winter in the Umpqua mountains, not being able to reach the settlements.

I would therefore recommend you to keep the old road. A better way may be found, but it is not best for men with wagons and families to try the experiment.

My remarks are brief, but I hope may prove beneficial to you.

Dated at Oregon City, this 22d of April, 1847.

GEO. ABERNETHY,
GOVERNOR OF OREGON TERRITORY AND
SUPERINTENDENT OF INDIAN AFFAIRS.

Governor George Abernethy of Oregon circulated advice to potential emigrants. Courtesy of Western Americana Collection, Beinecke Library, Yale University.

and the Continental Divide. Their deaths usually occurred as isolated incidents, not in wholesale "massacres." The only violence that lived up to that billing took place in southern Idaho, at the hands of the Bannock and Shoshone. But even so, some of the worst atrocities (mutilations and torture) were perpetrated by "white Indians," Caucasian robbers who hoped to shift blame for their crimes to the Indians, or by punitive expeditions organized by the military. The numerous instances of trouble initiated by white overlanders together with frequent cases of native assistance to people in distress contradict the stereotype of the savage Indian and virtuous pioneer.

The United States Army did not maintain a presence on the trail until 1849, the year Fort Vancouver was garrisoned, and some observers claimed that the troops caused more harm than good. Men frequently frustrated by the rules of what might be called "guerrilla" warfare were eager for battle and often treated peaceful Indians savagely. The army's random justice had the predictable effect of causing Indians to seek revenge on innocent emigrants.

If the military's contribution to the "winning" of Oregon in the conventional sense of fighting Indians was overstated, it nonetheless played a major part in early Northwest history through its underappreciated work of exploration. Federal interest in the Pacific Northwest during the early 1840s took the form of two military expeditions, one by sea, the other by land.

Lieutenant Charles Wilkes led a navy squadron to the South Pacific, to Antarctica, and ultimately to the

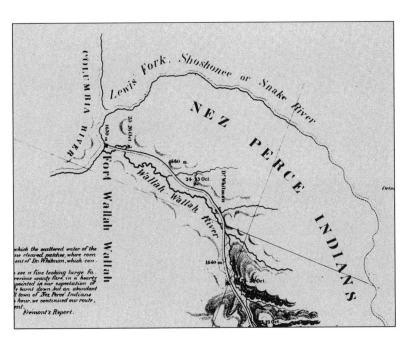

A detailed portion of Section 7 from the "Topographical Map of the Road from Missouri to Oregon . . ." based on the explorations of John C. Fremont. Published in 1845 with the emigrant in mind, Fremont's "trip-tik" was drawn at ten miles to the inch and contained references to distance from the start, Indian encampments, weather patterns, and the location of game, fish, and water.
Courtesy of Special Collections Division, University of Washington Libraries.

Northwest coast during a round-the-world voyage. In 1841, while Wilkes surveyed Puget Sound, one of his ships, the *Peacock,* on a mission to explore the Columbia River, ran afoul of the notorious bar at its mouth and sank. When Wilkes was finally able to report to Congress on his discoveries, the fate of the *Peacock* dramatized the importance of Puget Sound as the only truly safe harbor in the Oregon Country.

Wilkes's observation stiffened the resolve of American negotiators to reject British proposals that the Oregon Country be divided along the Columbia River. The extension of the United States boundary up to and along the forty-ninth parallel so as to include Puget Sound was in large measure a result of the Wilkes Expedition.

Also influential in the Americanization of Oregon were the reports of John C. Fremont. The "Great Pathfinder," as he was known, made use of the latest surveying technology and the narrative writing skills of his wife, Jessie Benton Fremont, to describe and publicize what he saw as an inviting West. Official reports of the Fremont explorations of 1842 and 1843–44 and the accompanying scientific cartography, including maps of the Oregon and California trails, provided valuable information to emigrants about distance, landmarks, river fords, and the disposition of native peoples. Fremont's work created a sensation that completely overshadowed the accomplishments of Wilkes and the navy survey in the popular mind and provided a very practical guide for Midwesterners aflame with "Oregon fever."

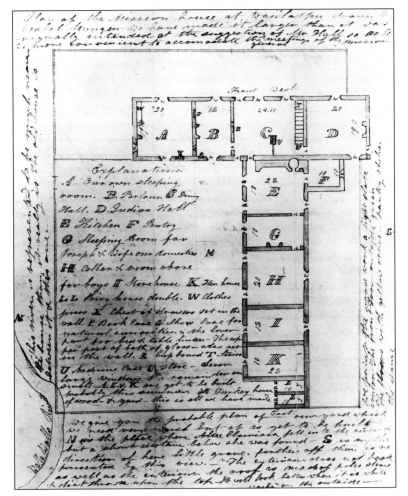

Narcissa Whitman's sketch of the famous mission at Waiilatpu contained in a letter (dated May 1840) to her brother Stephen Prentiss.
Courtesy of Oregon Historical Society.

A New Vision of the Northern West

Isaac Stevens is one of the better-known political figures from Washington's pioneer era, but his work as an explorer is often overlooked today. Stevens was appointed Washington Territory's first governor early in 1853, but he came west under the auspices of the War Department's Corps of Topographical Engineers. His assignment was to determine the feasibility of a northern route for a railroad to the Pacific.

The result of the first government expedition to follow Lewis and Clark was a detailed cartographic record of the northern West between the forty-seventh and forty-ninth parallels. The explorations of Stevens' engineers and officers, including George McClellan and John Mullan, resulted in the drawing of maps that made the earlier work of Lewis and Clark appear to be crude sketches.

Stevens also took care to remedy an omission in the entourage of Lewis and Clark. He hired John Mix Stanley, a famous painter of western Indian leaders, as the expedition's principal artist. Stanley prepared dozens of sketches of wilderness landscapes, trading posts, and native encampments which, when transformed into the lithographic plates that lavishly illustrated Stevens' monumental report, gave many Americans their first glimpse of the new western territories.

The lithographs offered rare views of the northern West as the explorer saw it. It was a world soon to fade into history with the coming of pioneer settlement.

Fort Okanogan, a Hudson's Bay Company fur trading depot, was situated at the confluence of the Okanogan and Columbia rivers. Stanley's drawing is the only known view of this early landmark. Courtesy of Special Collections Division, University of Washington Libraries.

In his sometimes eloquent geographical memoir, Stevens referred to Mount Baker, shown here, as the northwestern pillar of the United States. Courtesy of Washington State Capital Museum.

The scientific concerns of Stevens, Stanley, and their contemporary students of natural history can be read into this drawing of Kettle Falls, combining as it does the density of rock, the erosive power of water, and primal humans. Courtesy of Special Collections Division, University of Washington Libraries.

Cultures in Conflict

Chiefs at Dinner   Walla Walla Council 1855

Indian-white relations in the Pacific Northwest reached a low point in 1847 with the Whitman killing and the Cayuse War that followed, and they had already begun to decline again when Governor Isaac Stevens arrived on Puget Sound in 1853. Racial violence in southern Oregon, in the Columbia Gorge near the Dalles, and along the Oregon Trail had upset the peace that prevailed during the years of Hudson's Bay Company rule.

Acting upon the belief that agreements were needed before the territory was completely overrun with white settlers, Stevens rapidly sought to negotiate treaties with the Indians of Washington Territory.

Stevens began his treaty tour at Nisqually in December 1854. Although the

Governor Stevens went out of his way to ingratiate himself with the Nez Perce, who, as the most numerous and powerful tribe present at Walla Walla, held the diplomatic balance of power among the native people represented there. Here Gustavus Sohon shows the Stevens party's banquet held in honor of the visiting Nez Perce chiefs.
Courtesy of Washington State Historical Society.

Nisqually and Puyallup Indians ceded millions of acres of land, they retained, in the now famous language of the treaty, the "right of taking fish, at all usual and accustomed grounds and stations."

The governor next organized an expedition to eastern Washington to negotiate with the militarily formidable tribes of the Columbia Plateau. In an age

May. 1855. Walla Walla Council. Governor Stevens with Indians.

When the Walla Walla Council convened, Stevens addressed the native leaders arrayed before him in concentric circles. Note just to the right of center several Nez Perce scribes seated in a circle making their own transcript of the often tumultuous proceedings. Courtesy of Washington State Historical Society.

Kamayakhen

In this, the only known view of Yakima Chief Kamiakin, we see the most tragic figure arising out of the Stevens treaty tour. Kamiakin rejected the mantle of leadership Stevens imperiously bestowed upon him, only to be cajoled into signing a treaty. When many of the bands supposedly represented by Kamiakin attacked white miners and army troops, he was unfairly held responsible and led much of the rest of his life in semi-exile. Courtesy of Washington State Historical Society.

Colonel George Wright in command at the battle of Spokan Plain, September 5, 1858.
Drawing by Gustavus Sohon courtesy of Smithsonian Institution.

The closing festivities of the Walla Walla Council were as dramatic as its opening. Here Sohon recorded the Nez Perce scalp dance, held in part to welcome back their buffalo hunters from the Plains. In the scene depicted, a woman has broken through the circle of chiefs and warriors to treat a scalp from a recently fallen foe (hoisted on a pole) with ritual contempt. This dance, adapted from contacts with the Plains cultures, was a victory ceremony, not a preparation for war, and was usually led by a woman who had lost family members in combat. Courtesy of Washington State Historical Society.

before sophisticated photography, Stevens arranged to have a documentary artist, Private Gustavus Sohon, assigned to the treaty command.

Through his portraits of chiefs and warriors, Sohon compiled the only visual record of Stevens' epochal and often tumultuous treaty councils in eastern Washington.

As was true west of the Cascades, the native peoples of the Columbia Plateau resisted leaving their homes and living on reservations with their historic enemies. At the Walla Walla Council in 1855, the Cayuse, Umatilla, and Walla Walla peoples resisted moving to either Yakima or Nez Perce land. They secured from the governor the concession of a third reservation on the plateau.

Similarly, Chief Spokan Garry forced Stevens to promise to withdraw American troops from his district. Nonetheless, the governor's brusque manners and shortsighted policies during his treaty tour contributed in large measure to the outbreak of the so-called Yakima War.

A related conflict called the Spokane War occurred in 1858 when the army crossed the Snake River and violated the agreement made three years earlier with Spokan Garry. It ended after troops under the command of the often brutal Colonel George Wright forged a peace that lasted until the Nez Perce War of 1877.

The Walla Walla Council began in spectacular fashion with the arrival of the Nez Perce, who rode into the council grounds in a cavalcade over one thousand strong. Gustavus Sohon's drawing shows Governor Stevens and his party (at the foot of the flagpole) greeting Lawyer and the other principal Nez Perce chiefs while the warriors circle them in a parade meant both as tribute to the white leader and as a demonstration of strength. Courtesy of Washington State Historical Society.

Arrival of The Nez Perce Indians at Walla Walla Treaty May 1855

Arrival of The Nez Perce Indians To Wallawalla Treaty

Catholic Missions

Early Catholic missions in the Pacific Northwest had roots both in the United States and British North America. In the late 1830s French-speaking Catholic missionaries from Quebec came to minister to traders and trappers who worked for the Hudson's Bay Company along the Columbia River. In the early 1840s the Society of Jesus sent its members (known as Jesuits) to found missions among the natives of the northern Rocky Mountains.

Jesuit missionary activity in Washington began in 1845 with the founding of Saint Paul's Mission at Kettle Falls. Such early Roman Catholic "blackrobes" as Father Joseph Joset and Father Urban Grassi competed with Protestant missionaries to evangelize the native peoples.

Even after division of the Oregon Country in 1846, many Catholic missions in the far Northwest retained ties to the church in Quebec. For this reason the first community of Catholic religious women came from French-speaking Canada. They were the Sisters of Providence, led by Mother Joseph of the Sacred Heart, who arrived at Fort Vancouver in 1856. Mother Joseph and her small band of sisters founded schools and hospitals throughout the Northwest, and even as far afield as Alaska and southern California. It is perhaps a telling reminder of the importance of mission activity in Washington's history that the state's two representatives in Statuary Hall in Washington, D. C., are Marcus Whitman and Mother Joseph.

To support their charitable work, Sisters of Providence in the nineteenth century conducted annual "begging tours" to mining towns and logging camps throughout the Northwest. Courtesy of Sisters of Providence Archives, Seattle.

Saint Paul's Mission in Kettle Falls had stood empty for thirty-five years when this party visited the site in 1905. The church has been restored and is now maintained by the Washington Parks Department. Courtesy of Oregon Province Archives, Gonzaga University, Spokane.

The Evolution of Washington's Boundaries

Imagine a traveler leaving the Old Faithful Geyser Basin in Yellowstone National Park and encountering a sign that read "Welcome to Washington." Or consider a billboard that welcomed visitors to Spokane, the "Capital of the State of Columbia." Does Walla Walla, Oregon, sound strange? How about Olympia, British Columbia? These possibilities and others might have become reality had history taken a slightly different course.

When early overland parties crossed the Continental Divide near present-day Rock Springs, Wyoming, they entered Oregon Territory, although few would have celebrated at that point because their ultimate destination was still so far away. That part of Wyoming drained by the Snake River was added to Washington Territory in 1859 so that a more reasonably sized Oregon could be admitted as a state. Thus Washington at one time included part of the future Yellowstone National Park.

Residents of northern Idaho have often claimed that their state is the only one to have three capitals—Boise, Salt Lake City, and Spokane. The argument is frequently made that the whole Inland Northwest, from the Columbia River to the Rocky Mountains, should be a state of its own, with Spokane as the seat of government. That idea was first proposed in the 1860s.

The Walla Walla area was long a hotbed of secessionism. Prior to Spokane's emergence in the 1880s as the largest city on the Columbia Plateau, Walla Walla was the logical choice to become capital of a new inland territory or state. Political interests on Puget Sound were adamantly opposed to any division of Washington that left it without territory east of the Cascades. They feared a shrunken Washington could never be admitted to the Union or that it would simply be swallowed up by Oregon.

When Walla Walla failed to become the capital of a new territory during a gold rush in the early 1860s, some residents hoped to secede from the backwater territory of Washington and join the state of Oregon. After all, the Columbia River had long linked Walla Walla to Oregon settlements. Like all the others, this secession movement failed too.

The western and northern boundaries of Washington were determined by the Pacific Ocean and an international treaty. Great Britain insisted on the Columbia River as the permanent boundary between the two countries, while American diplomats favored a division that would keep Puget Sound in the United States. The British yielded on this point in the Oregon Treaty of 1846.

The Fourth of July thus became a more noteworthy occasion on Puget Sound than it might have been otherwise. It was during one such celebration in the early 1850s that several "northern Oregonians" from the Olympia area raised the prospect of splitting the Oregon Territory along the Columbia River. The people of Puget Sound were far from centers of population and government in the Willamette Valley and received few territorial benefits.

Most Oregonians living south of the Columbia River did not object, realizing that the sprawling territory was probably too large to be admitted as one state anyway. Settlers petitioned Congress to create a territory called "Columbia." Congress created the territory in March 1853, but not before two obscure Congressmen from the South amended the bill to change the name to Washington. They feared that since a District of Columbia already existed, a territory by the same name would cause confusion. So Washington Territory was named for the nation's first president.

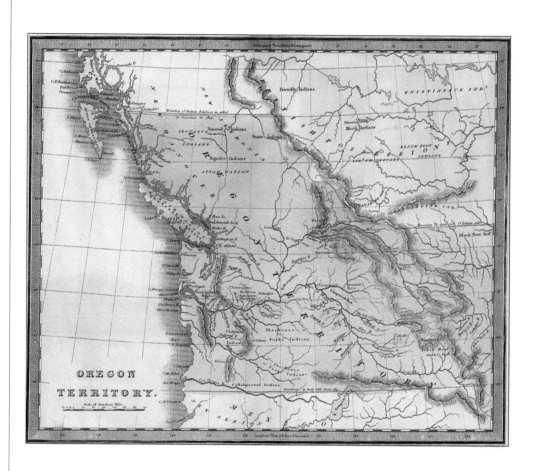

Above: The old Oregon Country stretched from the northern boundary of Mexican California to Russian Alaska and from the crest of the Rocky Mountains to the Pacific Ocean. It encompassed the future states of Washington, Oregon, and Idaho, plus western Montana, western Wyoming, and the southern two-thirds of British Columbia. Courtesy of Special Collections Division, University of Washington Libraries.

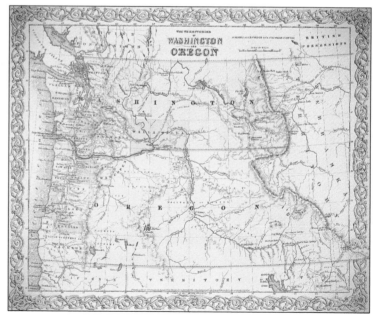

Right: This map reflects the division of the old Oregon Territory in order to create the new Washington Territory in 1853. Note that the eastern boundaries of both extended to the Continental Divide. Courtesy of Washington State Historical Society.

Few western territories ever got larger than their original size. Typically, several jurisdictions would be carved out of a larger one, as happened to Oregon. Washington Territory proved an exception in 1859 when Oregonians, thinking they could not be admitted to the Union in their enlarged state, had their eastern reach added to Washington. Courtesy of Special Collections Division, University of Washington Libraries.

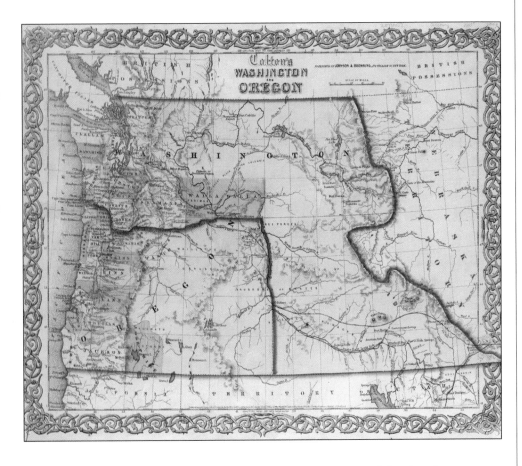

Until 1863, when the mining boom in the Clearwater District precipitated the creation of Idaho Territory, Washington could claim to be one of the largest territories in the west. That is ironic because stripping away Idaho made Washington (after its own admission in 1889) the smallest state west of the Mississippi. Courtesy of Special Collections Division, University of Washington Libraries.

Pioneer Settlers

Even as late as the turn of the century, pioneers, such as these from Grays Harbor County, were enduring the tribulations of homesteading in forested Washington.
Courtesy of Special Collections Division, University of Washington Libraries.

Monday 29. helth about the same. still and gloomy, nothing doing. Tuesday 30. still. helth on the gain. nothing a doing. dull."

Thus read two typical entries in the diary of Levi Lathrop Smith, cofounder of the pioneer settlement that grew into the community known as Olympia. Generations of Americans weaned on romantic accounts of the West would have difficulty identifying with Smith's hard life. From his diary, readers get a glimpse of real westering, which, with its descriptions of Smith busying himself gardening or building sheds, displays an extreme sense of loneliness.

There are perhaps other surprises in Washington's frontier past. Consider George Bush, a black pioneer who was one of the leaders of the first American party to settle on Puget Sound at New Market (Tumwater) in 1845. One of the most beloved men on the frontier, he often aided travelers passing his place on their way to a new start farther up the road.

Because federal law prohibited blacks from securing public land grants, Bush's friends in the territorial legislature successfully petitioned Congress for an exemption. Although black slavery was illegal in United States territories, there were several known instances of its

The descendants of George Bush, shown on their homestead south of Tumwater. Courtesy of Washington State Capital Museum.

existence; the government apparently choose not to enforce the ban. But slavery was a risky business in Washington because the Canadian border offered freedom to any slave who could cross it.

Women and men worked together in the "winning" of the Northwest's agricultural frontier. The Oregon Donation Land Act of 1850—which covered Washington lands—allowed families to obtain up to 640 acres because both husbands and wives were eligible for homesteads. Typical tasks for women included child rearing, food preparation, and regular contributions to field work.

In the early settlements like Olympia, Steilacoom, Seattle, and Bellingham, women took the lead in organizing social occasions and cultural institutions such as churches, clubs, schools, and balls. The development of rude frontier settlements into communities depended upon the organizing skills and consciousness of frontier women.

The noted early twentieth century photographer Darius Kinsey used an idiosyncratic Northwestern architectural form, a cedar stump house, as his trademark publicity piece. These stumps, a ubiquitous feature of the logging frontier, were used to store tools in the woods and as tourist attractions, and one served as a branch post office. Courtesy of Whatcom Museum of History and Art.

II: From Frontier to Urban-Industrial Society

The Great Northern Railway used Mount Index in the Washington Cascades as the subject for the cover of this 1920s-era promotional brochure. Courtesy of Richard Piper.

I f any act symbolized the taming of the Northwest frontier, it was the driving of the final spike to complete the nation's northern transcontinental railroad. In the 1840s, when the wagon ruts of the Oregon Trail were fresh, the overland trek from the Midwest to the Willamette Valley and Puget Sound required five or six months, a spirit of adventure, and endurance. By 1883, with the completion of a rail line linking Saint Paul to Puget Sound, a person could travel to remote Washington Territory in style and comfort in just five days.

For Washington, the three and one-half decades between the final spike and American entry into the First World War were a time of hurried catch-up. When the Civil War reduced Atlanta, Columbia, and Richmond to smoldering ruins, the communities of Seattle, Tacoma, and Spokane amounted to scarcely more than straggling villages. The rapid industrialization that left its mark on portions of the victorious North initially left Washington almost untouched. But that changed with a direct rail link to the East. It took Washington only a few years to accomplish an economic and social

A council of Crow Indians at the last spike ceremony near Garrison, Montana, in September 1883. The opening of the first direct rail line from Puget Sound to the East contributed to a decade of spectacular growth for Washington. Courtesy of Haynes Foundation Collection, Montana Historical Society.

evolution that had required several generations in the Eastern states.

In short, the key feature of the period from 1883 to 1917 was Washington's sometimes abrupt transition to the postfrontier world. On one side of that historical divide was the age of Lewis and Clark, the Whitmans, the Oregon Trail pioneers, and the Indian wars, and on the other was the urban-industrial age of transcontinental railroads, nationwide markets, commercial agriculture, large-scale industrial enterprise, colleges, and universities.

Before the end of the 1880s, two more transcontinental lines and a rail

Madden and Sargent's Saloon in Coulee City in 1891. The era's many saloons were the favorite targets of temperance reformers who deplored the connection between alcohol, prostitution, and political corruption. Courtesy of Haynes Foundation Collection, Montana Historical Society.

connection to California linked Washington to the larger world. Never before had its natural resources been so accessible to so many people.

Few aspects of life in Washington changed more dramatically during the transition years than patterns of settlement. Not only did the railroads make it easy for people to emigrate to the Northwest, they also actively recruited settlers. The promotional campaign greatly influenced population movement. During the decade of the 1880s, Oregon's

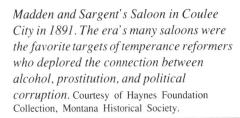

Photographer Frank Matsura photographed ranchers swimming their cattle across the Okanogan River in north-central Washington. Until the coming of the railroads, herds were driven across the Cascade Mountains to Seattle stockyards. Courtesy of Washington State University Library.

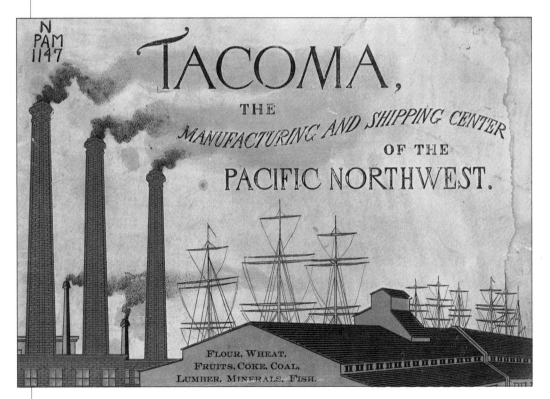

In an age innocent of problems caused by air pollution, promoters used smoking factories to advertise Tacoma's economic prosperity. Courtesy of Special Collections Division, University of Washington Libraries.

population grew by 80 percent while that of Washington grew by 380 percent. Few other states or territories in American history grew that fast during a single decade.

Newcomers poured into Washington in such great numbers that they altered prevailing patterns of life. They overwhelmed the power and influence of the pioneer generation. Many of the newcomers were foreign immigrants. In fact, no state or territory received more

Swedes and Norwegians in proportion to its already resident population than did Washington, which for years ranked third in the United States in Scandinavian population.

The population changes were most pronounced in urban areas. The 1880 census ranked Walla Walla as Washington's most populous community. But when the major railroads bypassed Walla Walla, Seattle sprinted ahead to claim first place, with a population of

In 1892 a fierce debate raged over whether the state flower should be clover or the western rhododendron. The state legislature ruled that only women could vote on the issue, and the rhododendron won, 7,704 votes to 5,720. Photograph by Tom Stilz courtesy of the photographer.

Western Washington's many tidal bays and rivers formed natural highways for dozens of ferryboats and passenger-carrying steamers like the sternwheeler Harbor Belle, *shown here in Grays Harbor at the turn of the century.* Courtesy of Washington State University Library.

forty-two thousand in 1890. During the decade of the 1880s, Seattle's population increased by 1,000 percent, Tacoma's by 3,000 percent, and Spokane's by an incredible 6,000 percent.

Headlong growth was not without its perils, however. A brief depression gripped Washington in the mid 1880s, and much longer and more severe hard times lasted from 1893 to 1897. Yet to many residents of Washington it seemed as if the events of a single day, July 17, 1897, dispelled the gloom and pessimism caused by four years of economic depression and social turmoil. On that long-remembered summer day, the Alaskan steamer *Portland* nosed into Seattle's Elliott Bay and brought news of an incredible gold find in the Canadian Yukon.

The trains that brought thousands of Klondikers to ports on Puget Sound occasionally brought seekers of another

The popular beaches and boardwalks along Seattle's Lake Washington could be reached by streetcar, and offered working people places to stroll, swim, and sip lemonade. This is the restaurant at Leschi Park in 1895. Courtesy of Museum of History and Industry.

In Aberdeen, Washington, high riggers dangle off a spar tree at an Independence Logging Company camp for photographer Clark Kinsey. Courtesy of Special Collections Division, University of Washington Libraries.

sort, people looking not for gold or glory but a chance to build a brave new world in the wilds of Washington. Utopias that bore such quaint names as Home, Equality, and Freeland arose on the shores of Puget Sound. Though they failed to turn Washington into a model socialist or anarchist commonwealth, the utopian colonies contributed to Washington's reputation for social and political innovation.

Encouraging the reformers was no less a figure than John R. Rogers, Washington's Populist governor from 1897 to 1901. As a third-party alternative to Republicans and Democrats, the People's or Populist Party was in the long run no more successful in Washington than

Lee Picket focused his camera on the main street of Skykomish in 1911.
Courtesy of Museum of History and Industry.

The smoke and the work of the mill dominated daily life in company towns. This photograph of the Puget Mill Company's sawmill and workers' housing at Port Ludlow was taken in June 1899. Courtesy of Special Collections Division, University of Washington Libraries.

elsewhere. But as a protest movement it provided an agenda for a later group of reform-minded Republicans and Democrats, who in the early twentieth century successfully turned many an innovative proposal into law. Perhaps the Populist Party's most lasting contribution was to make issues and individual candidates more important to the state's voters than party labels. It is no accident that independent-thinking politicians have flourished in Washington.

During the Progressive era of the early twentieth century, cities, states, and the federal government accepted greater responsibility for protecting citizens from a variety of dangerous or dishonest practices. Here Seattle weights and measures inspectors pose with confiscated scales, 1917. Photograph by James Lee courtesy of Special Collections Division, University of Washington Libraries.

Completion of the Northern Pacific Railroad, 1883

The first train from Saint Paul to Portland, September 8, 1883, opened a railway line from the Pacific Northwest to Lake Superior. Courtesy of Montana Historical Society.

A t Gold Creek in Montana Territory, several hundred politicians, bankers, railroad officials, investors, and journalists from the United States, Great Britain, and Germany gathered to celebrate the completion of a railroad linking the Great Lakes and Puget Sound. On September 8, 1883, the Northern Pacific Railroad opened the nation's second transcontinental line, the first built by a single company.

The person who presided over the final spike ceremony was Northern Pacific president Henry Villard, a handsome, genial man in his mid fifties. Villard believed his company's twenty-year struggle with nature and economic adversity merited spending the then enormous sum of a quarter of a million dollars to celebrate the final spike.

The festivities not only proved a great promotional success for the Northern Pacific but also signified the dawn of a

To facilitate construction of the Northern Pacific, Congress provided the railroad with a land grant that totaled several times the size of the New England states. In the late nineteenth century the Northern Pacific maintained an exhibition car to better acquaint prospective settlers with its landed domain. Courtesy of Montana Historical Society.

Trainloads of immigrants came west from Saint Paul to settle the great Northwest after the opening of the Northern Pacific line. Courtesy of Minnesota Historical Society.

new era for Washingtonians. The newness lay not in the railroad itself—local lines had existed in the territory since the 1860s—but in the direct and convenient connection it provided to the East. A journey that once required three to five months now only took five or six days. For investors and homeseekers no less than for residents who had arrived earlier by ship or covered wagon, an era of isolation had ended.

Newcomers poured into Washington by rail at a rate unimaginable only a decade earlier. Cities and farms transformed the landscape. Large-scale business enterprises, most notably the railroads, attained new prominence and power, and spurred the growth of organized labor. For Washington, the final spike ceremony divided a frontier past from an urban-industrial future.

No wonder Washingtonians celebrated the completion of the Northern Pacific in a manner later generations reserved for astronauts and Olympic champions.

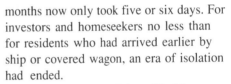

The territorial university, located at that time in downtown Seattle, welcomes Henry Villard. Ironically, Tacoma had already been selected as the Northern Pacific's western terminus. Courtesy of Museum of History and Industry.

Railroad-Made Washington

Early Washingtonians had a love-hate relationship with railroads, the agency that did most to shape the postfrontier world. They welcomed them to their communities believing that rail connections guaranteed prosperity and growth, and sulked when the twin ribbons of steel passed them by.

Would-be cities on Puget Sound fought bitterly with one another in the early 1870s to become the terminus of the Northern Pacific. The new town of Tacoma won the prize, but its smaller rival, Seattle, refused to concede, even though the Northern Pacific initially relegated it to the end of a branch line. Seattle's future looked considerably brighter after 1893 when it became the terminus of James J. Hill's Great Northern Railway.

By functioning as metropolitan corridors, railroads linked the towns and villages of Washington to Wall Street and Capitol Hill. Railroads not only opened the door to a nationwide market for local products—especially for bulky commodities like wheat and timber—but also increased the competition on Main Street, much to the dismay of local merchants. Traveling on business and visiting friends and relatives became easy, and if one went first class in one of the ornate sleeping cars, the journey might actually be pleasurable.

But this new freedom had its price, as Washingtonians became increasingly

Railroads made Seattle's turn-of-the-century waterfront a hub of activity. Courtesy of Special Collections Division, University of Washington Libraries.

Before the automobile, the railroad served as many a community's link to the outside world. In the early 1890s, when this photograph was taken, four trains a day linked the coal mining town of Franklin to Seattle, thirty-four miles distant. Courtesy of Museum of History and Industry.

PACIFIC BUSINESS COLLEGE. The Model Commercial College of the Coast. 320 Post St., S. F.

Washington—New Tacoma. 385
ALPHABETICALLY.

The Northern Pacific Railroad Company

HAS FOR SALE

2,000,000 ACRES of LAND

—— IN ——

WESTERN WASHINGTON,

Comprising Choice Agricultural and Timber Lands.

5,000,000 ACRES

—— IN ——

EASTERN WASHINGTON,

Suitable for Farming and Grazing.

Settlers desirous of making permanent homes will find here

A HEALTHFUL CLIMATE, FERTILE SOIL,

An intelligent and prosperous people,

A FIELD FOR VARIOUS INDUSTRIAL OCCUPATIONS,

SCHOOLS, CHURCHES,

And all the Advantages of a Civilized Community.

All the Company's land, except timber land, and such as may be valuable for other than agricultural purposes, will be sold to settlers at the Government Price of $2.50 per acre, for cash, with an addition of ten cents per acre to defray the cost of survey and conveyance.

FULL INFORMATION respecting the Country and Railroad and Government land may be had by addressing

LAND DEPARTMENT N. P. R. R. CO.,

New Tacoma, Washington Territory.

J. W. SPRAGUE,

General Superintendent.

25'

OLD PORT WINE, H. PALMER & CO., 302 Davis St., S. F.

W. A. & C. S. HOUGHTON, the leading Wholesale Booksellers of California, 615 J Street, Sacramento,

GRAY'S MUSIC STORE
The Largest Stock of American and Foreign Music, Musical Merchandise on the Coast Sand

To subsidize the building of the Northern Pacific, Congress provided the railroad with an enormous land grant. The railroad disposed of portions of its landed empire to raise funds and populate the countryside. Courtesy of Oregon Historical Society.

Students still traveled to college by train during the 1920s. Courtesy of Washington State University Library.

dependent on railroads. In the early 1890s, when Palouse farmers were unable to secure enough boxcars to haul their unusually heavy harvest of grain to market, they protested loudly.

The railroad could also bless or blight a community through freight rates. For years the citizens of Spokane complained that railroads charged more to ship goods from Chicago to Spokane than to Seattle, four hundred miles farther west.

Railroads shaped more than just the commerce of Washington. Railroads actively promoted settlement by distributing tens of thousands of elaborate, multicolored brochures in English, German, Norwegian, and other languages. They regularly ran homeseekers' specials and hauled immigrant families and their belongings at reduced rates. They fostered tourism and promoted national parks. The railroad station once functioned as a center of community life, civic showplace, and portal to all other destinations along the metropolitan corridor.

The Milwaukee Road electrified its line from Othello to Seattle and Tacoma and thereby advertised Washington's abundance of "white coal," or hydroelectric power. From 1911 until 1961, the railroad's deluxe passenger trains connected Puget Sound with Chicago. Courtesy of Washington State Historical Society.

Steamboats on Inland Waters

Water travel united many settlements in early Washington. In addition to the tall ships and steamers on Puget Sound, steamboats carried passengers, freight, supplies, and information to remote inland areas. The *Beaver,* a diminutive paddleboat constructed in England for the Hudson's Bay Company, inaugurated the Pacific Northwest's steamboat era in 1836. And the boats remained vital to the Inland Northwest until completion of the Northern Pacific Railroad in 1883.

Yet even after the coming of the railroads, steamboats continued to ply the waters of the Columbia and Snake rivers for several more decades. Rails and rivers often formed complementary parts of an integrated transportation system. Small railroads like Dorsey Baker's narrow-gauge line from Walla Walla to Wallula connected steamers on the Columbia River with inland settlements. Portage railroads at various points along the Columbia enabled river traffic to bypass unnavigable waters. Steamboating declined after the turn of the century as competing forms of transportation—barges, automobiles, and trains—took over its once crucial role.

Among the drawbacks of river transportation were numerous natural hazards including shoals, rapids, rocks, low water, and adverse weather. This 1917 photograph shows the steamer Spokane *trapped in January ice on the Snake River at Almota.* Courtesy of National Maritime Museum.

Sheep as well as people traveled by water. Here at Lake Chelan a flock crowds onto a steamer as passengers watch from above. By 1890, more than 825,000 sheep could be found grazing on the Columbia Plateau of eastern Washington. Courtesy of Museum of History and Industry.

Tall Ships on Puget Sound

Puget Sound, with its placid waters, sheltered inlets, and deep channels open twelve months a year, has long provided a natural harbor. Beginning in the 1850s, it served as a crossroads of the maritime world.

During the era of the tall ships, barks, schooners, sloops, brigs, and other vessels entered Puget Sound by way of Port Townsend, the customs station, to fill their holds with furs, timber, fish, grain, coal, and other Washington exports. Settlements grew rapidly at natural harbor sites. Port Townsend, Port Blakely, Port Ludlow, Tacoma, and Seattle all owed their existence to waterfront activities. Logging operations and sawmills, such as Henry Yesler's mill in Seattle, provided the foundations for emerging towns and

During the winter of 1905 Wilhelm Hester photographed these vessels—(left to right) 4-mast bark Englehorn, *4-mast bark* Bracadale, *3-mast bark* Albania, *4-mast bark* Wanderer, *4-mast schooner* Lyman D. Foster, *5-mast schooner* Crescent— *awaiting lumber cargo from the Port Blakely mills.* Courtesy of National Maritime Museum.

cities. A variety of languages could be heard on their streets as seamen from Hawaii, Chile, England, Japan, Germany, Australia, and other places took their shore leave. Frontier photographers like Wilhelm Hester captured the waterfront scene on film and sold prints of ships and their crews to members of this international community.

The crew of the 4-mast bark Lynton *posed on deck for Wilhelm Hester with Captain Edward Gates-James at lower left. Note the long chutes and tools that eased the loading of lumber.* Courtesy of National Maritime Museum.

In this unusual Puget Sound photograph, Captain Hiram Hudson Morrison (center) stands at the stern of his tugboat as it tows three vessels—(left to right) schooner Courtney Ford, *barkentine* Portland, *and schooner* Eric. Courtesy of National Maritime Museum.

Wilhelm Hester also captured the interior of the Lynton *on film. In sharp contrast to the disorder on deck, the well-maintained and lavishly adorned shipmaster's cabin offered Captain and Mrs. Gates-James a Victorian refuge while away from home.* Courtesy of National Maritime Museum.

Wheat Harvest

Washington agriculture is as diverse as the state's environment: dairy farms in Whatcom County, sheep ranches in Grant County, apple orchards in Chelan County, vineyards in Benton County. The list goes on. Today over sixty crops are grown within the state's boundaries. During most years of the twentieth century, however, no agricultural commodity contributed more to the Washington economy than wheat, and its harvest has long been a favorite subject of photographers.

Before 1914, horses or mules provided the power needed to plow, cultivate, seed, and harvest the winter wheat. Even with machinery it was a labor-intensive process that once required more than 106 total worker-hours to harvest one hundred bushels of wheat. With the appearance of the combine and gradual refinements to adapt it to the hilly Palouse, labor requirements were drastically reduced. Improved varieties of grain, technological innovations that ranged from gasoline-powered machinery to bulk shipment by truck and barge, and an increase in farm sizes transformed the wheat industry in the twentieth century.

The ever-changing tapestry of farm and ranch land, and the drama of the Palouse harvest, have long inspired photographers like Asahel Curtis. With his camera Curtis captured more than fifty thousand images of the Evergreen State. Courtesy of Special Collections Division, University of Washington Libraries.

Harvesting Large Acreages of Wheat in Washington, with combined Harvester and Thresher
F. A. MILLER, Gen. Pass. Agt., C. M. & St. P. Ry., O. E. SHANER, Immigration Agt., 750 Marquette Bldg., Chicago
GEO. W. HIBBARD, Gen. Pass. Agt., C. M. & P. S. Ry., Seattle, Wash.

A combine in the rolling Palouse country near Endicott in 1938. It was called a "combined" harvester because the machine both cut and threshed the grain. The first combines were pulled by large teams of horses or mules; later machines were self-propelled.
Courtesy of Washington State University Library.

A stationary steam threshing machine in the shadow of Steptoe Butte in the early twentieth century. This was the busiest place on any ranch during the harvest.
Courtesy of Washington State University Library.

The Pacific Coast Elevator near Thornton in 1898. Until the Second World War, much of Washington's wheat was shipped to market in burlap sacks. The backbreaking work of filling and sewing shut each 130-pound sack required an army of migratory harvest hands.
Courtesy of Washington State University Library.

Timber!

A log raft being assembled in Stella in 1896. Such rafts were used to transport logs from the lower Columbia River to sawmills as distant as San Diego, California. Courtesy of Oregon Historical Society.

I t is hard to imagine an economic activity more closely associated with the Evergreen State than logging. In 1910, when Washington was the nation's number one lumber producing state, 63 percent of its wageworkers depended upon the forest products industry for jobs.

The economy of many early coastal towns depended on the extensive forests that surrounded them. Pioneer settlers on Puget Sound denuded the hillsides along its shores to make lumber, boxes, doors, wooden pipe, and chairs. Beginning in the 1850s, they sent much of this production to California, which provided an important market for Northwest timber transported by tall ship. Even after the completion of the Northern Pacific Railroad, Washington timber continued to

Loggers moved a heavy steam donkey to a new location by attaching a cable to a tree and using the machine to move itself slowly overland. Courtesy of D. Kinsey Collection, Whatcom Museum of History and Art.

One of many temporary communities that once dotted the woods of Washington.
Courtesy of Special Collections Division, University of Washington Libraries.

be shipped predominantly by water. In 1897, 124 million board feet of Washington timber went by land but 440 million board feet went by sea. Half a decade later, with favorable freight rates offered by the Great Northern and other transcontinental railroads, the emphasis shifted to overland transportation.

Early logging operations were frequently family-run or small-scale business enterprises. But during the 1890s, investors from the Great Lakes region, whose timber supplies were being depleted rapidly, looked to Washington

Transporting logs from the woods to market often required the construction of roads, flumes, trestles, and railroads. Clark Kinsey photographed an Asian railroad construction gang at work for the Schafer Bros. Lumber & Shingle Company. Courtesy of Special Collections Division, University of Washington Libraries.

Topping a spar tree, probably the most dramatic logging job, draws a crowd at a Clear Lake Lumber Company camp in 1919. Courtesy of Library of Congress.

for future income. In a much-publicized deal in 1900, Frederick Weyerhaeuser purchased 900,000 acres of Northwest forest land from his Saint Paul, Minnesota, neighbor, the rail baron James J. Hill. This signaled the consolidation of the logging industry into the hands of a few and the beginning of the great era of Washington timber production.

During the nineteenth century, timbermen paid little attention to the protection of their resource. But after a 1902 fire burned two billion board feet of timber in Washington and Oregon, they became more conscious of the need to conserve and protect their commodity. Public and private forest fire associations worked together to establish industrywide controls.

This postcard depicting "Washington Toothpicks" was probably used to impress friends back East. Courtesy of Special Collections Division, University of Washington Libraries.

A team of oxen pulled logs down a "skid road" to the water's edge. Special tallow was used to grease the skids. Courtesy of Museum of History and Industry.

Burning stumps to clear logged-off land near Sumner. Courtesy of Washington State University Library.

Stump Farmers

Engaging in what was almost an agricultural sideshow were Washington's stump farmers, a hearty but inevitably impoverished lot who had the energy and optimism to spend countless hours blasting and pulling stumps in an attempt to convert infertile patches of logged-off land into pastures and fields.

This movement attracted most attention during the first quarter of the twentieth century when logged-off lands were widely but mistakenly promoted as a panacea for urban congestion and poverty.

Sawmills

The factory side of big timber has always suffered in comparison to the presumed "romance" of the logger's life. The latter had a hard life—traveling from camp to camp, often living on food of poor quality and sleeping in beds infested with vermin—but their conquest of the forest was glorified through photography. Images of loggers reposing in the undercut of gargantuan trees are to the early twentieth century Northwest what exotic fur traders and Indian warriors were to the nineteenth century—stereotypical views of the wild and resource-rich West.

Millworkers rarely attracted the cameras of the mythmakers, although they were as vital to bringing finished woodwork to the market as any "high rigger."

If conditions in backwoods logging camps contributed to the reformist, and often radical, spirit of the times, conditions in the mills did likewise. In 1917, *Sunset* magazine graphically portrayed one of the most hazardous jobs on Washington's industrial frontier: shingle weaving.

"Shingle weaving is not a trade; it is a battle. For ten hours a day the sawyer faces two teethed steel disks whirling around two hundred times a minute. To the one on his left he feeds heavy blocks of cedar, reaching over with his left hand to remove the rough shingles it rips off. He does not, cannot stop to see what his left hand is doing.

A shingle "weaver" at work. At his left is an upright shingle sawing or "weaving" machine. In front and to the right is a jointer, which reduces a shingle to uniform width and square edges. Courtesy of Washington State Historical Society.

After shingle weavers toss their work into chutes, the packers below them prepare the product for market. Courtesy of Washington State Historical Society.

His eyes are too busy examining the shingles for knot holes to be cut out by the second saw whirling in front of him.

"The saw on his left sets the pace. If the singing blade rips fifty rough shingles off the block every minute, the sawyer must reach over to its teeth fifty times in sixty seconds; if the automatic carriage feeds the odorous wood sixty times into the hungry teeth, sixty times he must reach over, turn the shingle, trim its edge on the gleaming saw in front of him, cut out the narrow strip containing the knot hole with two quick movements of his right hand and toss the completed board down the chute to the packers, meanwhile keeping eyes and ears open for the sound that asks him to feed a new block into the untiring teeth. Hour after hour the shingle weaver's hands and

A dry shingle storage shed is visited by an inspector. Courtesy of Washington State Historical Society.

arms, plain unarmored flesh and blood, are staked against the screeching steel that cares not what it severs. Sooner or later he reaches over a little too far, the whirling blade tosses drops of red into the air and a finger, hand, or part of an arm comes sliding down the chute."

Fishing and Canning

Although often overshadowed by the timber industry, fishing and canning were among Washington's first commercial activities. Early accounts expressed amazement at the numbers of fish swimming along the coast, through the Strait of Juan de Fuca, around Puget Sound, and up the river systems that reached far inland. Indians traded and sold fish to explorers and settlers, and during the years before statehood, they caught most of the fish that were for sale. The first commercial cannery opened on the Columbia River in 1866, and eleven years later one started on Puget Sound at Mukilteo, but fishing and canning were not yet highly developed industries.

Commercial fishing expanded rapidly during the last two decades of the 1800s; the dollar value of Washington's fishing industry multiplied thirtyfold between 1880 and 1902. By 1908, the value of Washington fish products was surpassed only by three other states, all on the East Coast. Just before the First World War, the state produced twenty million dollars' worth of fish and shellfish.

Raising a filled salmon trap. Photograph by Asahel Curtis courtesy of Special Collections Division, University of Washington Libraries.

Asahel Curtis photographed these Anacortes workers treating a net with bluestone, about 1938. Courtesy of Special Collections Division, University of Washington Libraries.

Fishermen adapted their gear to the season and the place, evolving highly efficient fishing methods. By 1880 they had developed the still common technique of purse seining, in which nets form a large circle around entire schools of fish. An older method used gill nets, which entangled the fish. In some places, especially along the Columbia River, men or horses dragged nets along the beach. Many items of equipment that the fishermen used a century ago are now illegal—the rotary scoop called a fish wheel, and permanent seines, traps, or pound nets.

Other technological changes, including motor-powered boats and mechanized canning, made it possible to catch and preserve an immense number of fish. Improved methods increased the catch and the depth of the nets, reaching the large salmon that swam well below the surface. In 1903, the year the first motorized fishing boat appeared on Puget

These workers were photographed unloading, or "brailing," salmon from a fish trap in 1913. The device, one of several different kinds of equipment ultimately declared illegal, gave fishermen the advantage over the abundant salmon of Puget Sound and the Washington coast. Courtesy of Library of Congress.

Chinese workers so predominated in certain stages of the canning process that whites commonly called the most significant mechanized canning device the "iron chink." These men were photographed at a cannery weighing machine in 1913. Courtesy of Library of Congress.

Publicity photographs like this emphasized the seemingly endless supply of fish available to the Washington salmon industry. Photograph by Asahel Curtis courtesy of Museum of History and Industry.

Sound, a canning machine was invented that cleaned and scraped sixty to eighty-five salmon a minute.

Immigrant men and women did most of the hard labor involved in fishing and canning. Arriving in Washington without money, Slavs, Scandinavians, and Chinese worked side by side in the canneries. Greeks and other immigrants who had fished in their native countries worked in the fishing fleets in Washington as well.

The damming of the Columbia River permanently altered Washington fishing. Fish ladders and elevators at some dams allowed fish to continue upriver to spawn, but at others, including the huge Grand Coulee Dam completed in 1941, the law requiring them was not enforced and no ladders were built. Grand Coulee's construction barred salmon from 1,100 linear miles of streams and is believed to have caused a sudden and dramatic reduction of salmon in lower Puget Sound.

Government agencies have long attempted to counteract the effects of dam building, water pollution from mill contamination and municipal sewage, and the destruction of salmon spawning beds by poor logging practices. Artificial propagation and conservation efforts began soon after statehood, when the Department of Fisheries began to regulate fishing and build hatcheries. By 1908, state facilities operated on Puget Sound, Willapa Harbor, Grays Harbor, and the Columbia River. More recently the Northwest Power Act of 1980 proposed to restore fish populations damaged by hydroelectric development. Whether it can actually do so remains to be seen.

But even with increased mitigation efforts, salmon and steelhead trout still face many life threats, including the lack of genetic diversity that makes salmon vulnerable to diseases that occasionally kill millions of them while they are still in the hatchery.

Men and women of all races and nationalities worked together at this "sanitary filling machine" in 1913. Courtesy of Library of Congress.

Black Diamonds

The reign of King Coal in Washington was short but significant. Coal was discovered in the Cascade foothills east of Puget Sound in the 1860s. By 1883 Wilkeson, Carbonado, and Newcastle had become the largest and most boisterous mining towns in the territory. Sailing ships carried coal from the docks of Seattle, Tacoma, and Bellingham to customers in California and across the Pacific.

Toward the end of the 1880s the Northern Pacific Railroad opened new mines at Roslyn, on the east side of the Cascades, that soon surpassed the largest mines west of the mountains. By 1905 the Northern Pacific employed more than two thousand miners and produced 51 percent of the coal in the state. That helped to make Washington the second largest source of coal in the western United States.

Like most coal towns in the eastern United States, those of Washington were characterized by their isolation, company housing, and the proverbial company store. Many early Cascade miners had

Coal miners with loaded trips near Renton. Courtesy of Washington State Historical Society.

At the Newcastle mine, located east of Lake Washington, workers sort slate and other impurities from coal in 1902. Photograph by Asahel Curtis courtesy of Washington State Historical Society.

become familiar with unionism in the mines of the East or abroad. Their concern for mine safety prompted one of the earliest strikes in Washington, a bitter seven-month struggle at Newcastle in the spring of 1886 that was marked by violence and the declaration of martial law.

During the late 1880s serious industrial violence erupted several more times in the coal fields. Strife provoked by professional strike breakers led the framers of Washington's state constitution to ban private armies.

Washington's coal production peaked during the second decade of the twentieth century. Largely as a result of competition from California oil, coal production entered a long decline after the First World War and never recovered.

The Carbonado mines, seen here in 1883, were located in the foothills west of the Cascade Range. Courtesy of Haynes Foundation Collection, Montana Historical Society.

Shipbuilding

Shipbuilders were easily attracted to Puget Sound for its protected harbors and tall timbers at the water's edge. Wooden schooners, steamers, and sternwheelers built at Port Ludlow, Port Blakely, and Port Orchard plied Pacific waters for decades. The modern shipbuilding industry, however, was a direct result of military spending, not individual entrepreneurship.

Bremerton became home to the Puget Sound Naval Shipyard in 1891. It was "ideally located," the secretary of the navy reported in 1907, with water deep enough "to float the navies of the world. The government has undoubtedly received full value for every dollar expended on this yard." Still, it was unable to produce all the ships needed to fight the First World War, and federal funds had to be used to build or improve private shipyards in Seattle, Tacoma, and Vancouver.

The largest of those was the Skinner and Eddy operation in Seattle. Between 1915 and 1916, the number of men employed in Seattle shipyards climbed from two hundred to six thousand. By 1919, forty-one shipyards in Washington and Oregon had received $458 million to provide 297 vessels for the war effort.

The Second World War required a similar expansion of the industry. Shipyards in Seattle, Tacoma, Bremerton, Vancouver, and Grays Harbor produced an armada of destroyers, cargo ships, and aircraft carriers. Puget Sound Naval Shipyard at Bremerton, which boasted the largest facility on the West Coast, repaired crippled ships from Pearl Harbor as well as constructed new ones.

This Asahel Curtis photograph gives a sense of the scale of wooden-hulled construction at the Hall Brothers shipyard, Port Blakely, about 1903. Courtesy of Museum of History and Industry.

In this 1916 photograph, taken at the Matthews Ship Yard in Hoquiam, wooden-hulled ships sit in various stages of construction. Courtesy of Museum of History and Industry.

Seattle took special pride in the battleship Nebraska, *launched in 1904 at the Moran Brothers shipyard. It is pictured here in the dry dock at the Puget Sound Naval Shipyard.* Courtesy of Museum of History and Industry.

The First World War brought prosperity to the Seattle shipbuilding industry. Federal funds financed new shipyard construction to provide modern, steel-hulled ships like those being built here, at the Ames Shipbuilding Company, 1918. Courtesy of Museum of History and Industry.

The Wageworkers' Frontier

Washington in the late nineteenth century offered an abundance of seasonal wage labor to willing workers. There were jobs for loggers, miners, fishermen, millworkers, and migratory farm hands. Construction workers of all types were needed to build the Northwest's rapidly expanding network of railway lines and growing villages and cities.

Often the workers were single and lived in bunkhouses and ate in tents, or they rented rooms in boarding houses. They did dangerous work for low wages; they labored in the rain or sun for long hours. The homebodies among them eventually found stable employment, put down roots, and raised families; but "bindle stiffs" moved from job to job and formed a society apart from conventional family and

Workers in the McConnell Grain Warehouse in Pullman around 1895. Courtesy of Washington State University Library.

Asahel Curtis posed the morning shift at the Pacific Coast Coal Company in Newcastle for this 1909 photograph. Coal was first discovered here in 1863. Courtesy of Special Collections Division, University of Washington Libraries.

In their time off, single wageworkers congregated in camp eating halls to amuse themselves with cards and beer. Courtesy of Museum of History and Industry.

Construction workers pause from blasting a railroad tunnel through the Cascades at Snoqualmie Pass to pose in their cramped and dirty working space with their boss in 1913. Photograph by H. English courtesy of Special Collections Division, University of Washington Libraries.

neighborhood life.

The wageworkers' frontier in Washington was ever in a state of flux. It expanded as new agricultural lands and timber and mining camps opened, and contracted when older camps were abandoned with the depletion of natural resources, or, as infrequently happened, when one of the raw, socially unstable communities survived and matured. In 1870 day labor existed primarily in scattered fish canneries, tidewater sawmills, and flour mills. The wageworkers' frontier continued to grow after the construction of Washington's railroad network in the early twentieth century, then rapidly faded away following the First World War.

Loggers—and the cooking crew—from Camp #2 of the Clemens Log Company posed for this photograph by Clark Kinsey. Courtesy of Special Collections Division, University of Washington Libraries.

Women at Work

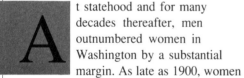

In areas where they were excluded from wage work, enterprising women earned money by doing traditional domestic labor for pay—cooking, cleaning, and running boarding houses for the men of the wageworkers' frontier, or establishing laundries like this one, serving the gold miners of Republic in about 1899. Courtesy of Eastern Washington State Historical Society.

At statehood and for many decades thereafter, men outnumbered women in Washington by a substantial margin. As late as 1900, women comprised only 36 percent of Seattle's population and 43 percent of Spokane's. Most jobs on the wageworkers' frontier were restricted to men. With the exception of the canning industry, which offered employment in the traditionally female field of food processing, Washington industry held little opportunity for women. Many women did work for money, however, earning it by doing domestic labor for male workers.

In frontier settlements, women made their families' clothing, kept poultry and dairy animals, raised vegetables, and did the cooking and laundry without benefit of gas, electricity, or running water. In

mining, milling, and logging towns, they entered the cash economy doing those same chores for strangers. Married women took in laundry and sewing, or kept boarders; their boarding houses often became the town restaurant and hotel. Unmarried women might cook meals and wait tables in bunkhouses and boarding houses, wash clothes at commercial laundries, or work as dance hall girls or prostitutes.

As the cities grew, new employment opportunities for women arose. Department stores hired salesclerks, offices employed stenographers and typists, and the expanding telephone exchanges needed operators. Although those indoor occupations were relatively clean, workers there, as in the canneries and laundries, worked long hours for low wages.

The women working for the Seattle long distance exchange in 1902 served the city's four thousand telephones. Courtesy of Museum of History and Industry.

Reform-minded legislators enacted employment restrictions for women soon after the turn of the century—the eight-hour day for females in any "mechanical or mercantile establishment, laundry, hotel, or restaurant" in 1911, and a minimum wage for women in 1915.

Many women found employment in the industries that mechanized their traditional task of food preparation. These workers dressed razor clams for the Pioneer Packing Company in Copalis in 1915. Courtesy of Special Collections Division, University of Washington Libraries.

These cannery workers were photographed at the Apex Fish Company in 1913; cannery operations on Puget Sound peaked that year with an output of 2.5 million 48-pound cases of salmon. Photograph by Asahel Curtis courtesy of Special Collections Division, University of Washington Libraries.

An Ethnic Mosaic

E thnic histories, festivals, and other social and educational activities have created a new version of our state's past. Not too long ago, history books portrayed ethnic and minority groups in cameo roles—the French-Canadian trapper, for instance—or in the case of native peoples, only as a backdrop for the westward movement of emigrant whites. The contribution of Hispanics to Washington's heritage has often been treated like bookends to the main shelf of history. There is mention of Spanish explorers on the Pacific Coast during the great era of exploration, and then, much later, some discussion of how a labor shortage during the Second World War brought the first large Hispanic migration to the fields of eastern Washington. The full dimension of an ethnic group's heritage is lost in that way.

Ethnic diversity in Washington resulted in large measure from the policies and actions of the Northern Pacific Railroad, the Great Northern Railway, and other

transcontinental railroads. They encouraged the employment of Chinese construction workers in Washington and opened the way for other racial and ethnic groups to follow. Coal companies that were often railroad subsidiaries imported black miners from the East to work in the underground fields of King and Kittitas counties. Immigrants from all corners of Europe—notably Great Britain, Italy, Russia, and Sweden—populated the farms and factories that sprang up all over Washington between 1883 and 1920. In 1910 only a fifth of Washington's population was native to the state; half was foreign born.

Scandinavians formed the largest of the incoming ethnic groups. King, Pierce, and Spokane counties typically had the greatest concentrations of ethnic groups, although there were some anomalies, such as the Italians in Kittitas County, or the Finns, Swedes and Norwegians along the shores of Grays Harbor.

Of course, not all immigrant experiences were the same during this period of Washington's economic maturation. Consider the different male/female ratios in Washington in 1910

An immigrant entrepreneur at Port Blakely. Courtesy of Museum of History and Industry.

Members of the immigrant Rosellini family went on to great prominence in Washington history, including the governorship. Courtesy of Washington State Historical Society.

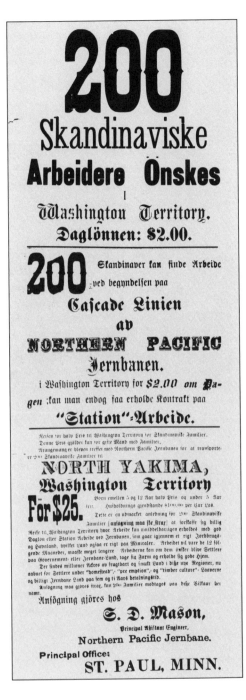

The close relationship between European immigration and railroad promotion is revealed in this advertisement. Courtesy of Minnesota Historical Society.

gang labor.

The table below compares the family sizes of two immigrant groups in Washington at the time of the 1930 census.

In family size, as in many other aspects of life, the differing cultural patterns of Washington's ethnic peoples are clear.

Number of children	4,836 Italian families	4,639 Finn families
1	649	643
2	644	990
3	773	1126
4	920	856
5	768	489
6	497	245
7	266	145
8	169	63
9	150	82

for the following groups of people:

Native born	120/100
English	177/100
Swedish	188/100
Italian	544/100
Chinese	1326/100.

Those figures tell the tales of whole families being unable to afford passage to America; of differing or abnormal family life patterns; of single people or husbands preparing the way for others; of migratory

Blacks held many service jobs with the transcontinental railroads during their passenger-carrying heyday. Courtesy of Washington State Historical Society.

Indian Worlds Old and New

"History" happened fast in the far Northwest. Changes that took place over centuries in the East or South occurred in Washington in a matter of decades. The clearest way to see how rapidly Euro-American civilization achieved preeminence in the Northwest is to view change from the perspective of a Native American in 1877.

With the conclusion that year of the often romanticized Nez Perce War, native armed resistance to white encroachment in the Northwest ended. A seventy-five-year-old Nez Perce woman or man would have seen or met the explorer, fur trader,

Indian education at the turn of the century reflected the same currents driving the crafts movement popularized for black Americans by Booker T. Washington. These Quinault Indian boys are working on a carpentry project at Taholah. Courtesy of Washington State Historical Society.

A blacksmith's shop was one of the principal commitments made by the federal government to Indian nations agreeing to treaties and reservations. Shown here are two workers positioned at the front of the shop at the Indian Agency at Nespelem, with Cayuse/Nez Perce brands emblazoned on the door. Photograph by Dr. Edward H. Latham courtesy of Eastern Washington State Historical Society.

missionary, treaty maker, gold seeker, and farmer-settler. The era of each followed quickly upon the last. Within a single generation, people born in the precontact cultures of the Columbia Plateau lived to witness the extermination of the buffalo, the filling up of their land with settlers, and the confinement of many Indians to reservations.

In the post–Civil War reservation era most Indians altered their lives to fit new and difficult circumstances. Some Native Americans became self-sufficient agrarians—a few in eastern Washington maintained continuity with their cultural heritage by acquiring large herds of horses and cattle—while others worked on the farms of whites. Still more moved to hamlets and larger cities to find work in the maturing industrial economy.

Probably the most wrenching cultural transition took place at the mission or

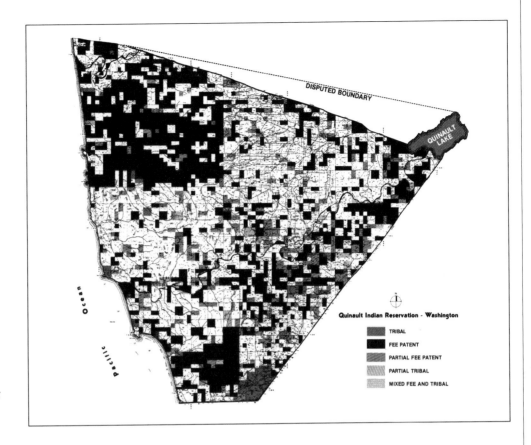

A map of the Quinault Reservation, showing that nearly one-third of the trust land is owned by non-Indian individuals or firms, reveals the deleterious effect of the Dawes Severalty Act on Washington's twenty-six reservations. Courtesy of Quinault Indian Nation.

government Indian school, where young people were subjected to forced acculturation. The religious and civil authorities who ran the schools always presumed that assimilation into the white way of life was both desirable and possible. While some Indians appeared to assimilate, native people were actually trapped between the old life and the new.

All the while, what remained of their material patrimony—lands reserved for their exclusive use and the right to fish or hunt "at all usual and accustomed places"—was constantly being eroded by outright subterfuge or social engineering. Particularly devastating was the Dawes Severalty Act that Congress passed in 1887. Although reformist in spirit, it favored settlers who coveted choice Indian lands.

The Dawes Act allowed reservations, formerly held in common by the whole tribe, to be broken into individual allotments. Over time many Indians lost their land, either through shortsighted sale to whites, failure to pay taxes, or through disuse, having chosen or been forced to

settle on unproductive soil.

The effect of the allotment system on Indian trust lands can be observed by a close inspection of any reservation map. The checkerboard pattern contrasting native and white holdings reveals the legacy of a nineteenth century experiment gone awry.

Three Spokane Indian children, circa 1908. The Spokane Indian reservation was one of the last reservations created on the plateau. Courtesy of Eastern Washington State Historical Society.

Cities and Towns in the Wilderness

This is the first known view of Washington's capital city, Olympia, shortly after its founding by L. L. Smith. The sketch by James M. Alden dates from the U.S. coast survey of the 1850s.
Courtesy of Washington State Historical Society.

Building their homes against steep mountainsides and in dense forests, Washington townsfolk fashioned their lives and their communities. They built quickly at first, erecting wooden shelters—plain buildings made from readily available materials—to protect them from rain and snow. In 1870, their towns were still small. Walla Walla, with a population of 1,394, was the largest in the territory, followed by Olympia (1,203) and Seattle (1,107).

During the years before statehood, the population of all of those towns, and that of the territory as a whole, mushroomed from 23,955 in 1870 to 357,232 in 1890. Settlers continued to arrive from the East, and immigrants came from foreign countries as diverse as Norway and China. Some, such as the Odessa Germans, formed towns of their own; others, such as the eastern Europeans of Tacoma, formed communities within larger cities. A group

Low down payments, a timeless come-on used to sell building lots in early Spokane.
Courtesy of Eastern Washington State Historical Society.

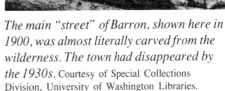

The main "street" of Barron, shown here in 1900, was almost literally carved from the wilderness. The town had disappeared by the 1930s. Courtesy of Special Collections Division, University of Washington Libraries.

This view of Leavenworth, taken in 1912, gives a sense of the physical presence of mountains in so many Washington towns and cities. Courtesy of Library of Congress.

of blacks brought in as strikebreakers in 1888 stayed in Roslyn; other blacks settled in Seattle and Spokane.

People came because there was money to be made—manual labor for the poor and financial opportunities for people with money to invest. Speculators, many representing wealthy Easterners, invested in the land company that started Everett in 1888 when James J. Hill talked of making that town the Puget Sound terminus for his Great Northern Railway. The Northern Pacific Railroad brought prosperity to Tacoma.

James Glover was one of several

speculators who sought to capitalize on the completion of a railroad. Along with his partners he purchased land for a townsite at the falls of the Spokane River in 1873. By the time the Northern Pacific arrived ten years later, 350 other individuals had staked their future in the settlement known as Spokane Falls. The town boomed, growing in population to twenty-six thousand by 1890. Not every investment or town was as dynamic or successful as Spokane, Tacoma, or Seattle, but each community in carving out its place contributed to the transformation of the territory into a state.

The wide main street of Rosalia in May 1889 was typical of many agricultural centers built in the eastern part of Washington. False fronts on the stores were designed to make the buildings appear more substantial than they really were. Courtesy of Haynes Foundation Collection, Montana Historical Society.

Promoting the Promised Land

P eople of the North, East, South and West, take my advice, go and make your Home in Wonderful Washington. The climate is pleasant, free from cold, and perfectly healthy. There are splendid opportunities for both Labor and Capital."

Those words from a typical nineteenth century promotional brochure lauded the virtues of "Wonderful Washington," attracting both settlers and investors to the state. A virtual mountain of colorful fliers, circulars, guidebooks, and maps produced by private investors, railroad land departments, local chambers of commerce, and other organizations helped push Washington's population to well over one million residents by 1910.

The literature attempted to attract, as one circular phrased it, "the very best kind of immigrants . . . people with brains, money and enterprise." In addition to printed materials, fairs and expositions sought to advertise the state.

Those efforts followed a tradition of promotional activities in the Pacific Northwest. News of the possibilities of early Washington came from printed materials such as James G. Swan's *The Northwest Coast; or Three Years' Residence in Washington Territory,* published in 1857. Asa Shinn Mercer, Elwood Evans, and Ezra Meeker all published similar accounts recording the benefits of the far Northwest.

As territorial governor and head of a

Promotional literature, such as this Northern Pacific Railroad brochure, relied on photographs as well as text to present the strongest case to potential settlers and investors. Courtesy of Minnesota Historical Society.

After the Northern Pacific Railroad bypassed Seattle and chose Tacoma as its terminus, Seattle citizens worked to create a rival "Grand Territorial Road" from their own city to Walla Walla. As part of the ultimately unsuccessful scheme, they established a "Grand Lottery" to attract settlers and finance the road. Courtesy of Special Collections Division, University of Washington Libraries.

federal railroad survey, Isaac I. Stevens was another of the region's tireless promoters. Disputing earlier negative reports on the lands east of the Cascades, he described the potential of the various environments in his official report. "When this interior becomes settled there will be a chain of agricultural settlements all the way from the Walla Walla to the Dalles," he predicted.

Pullman promoted itself as the commercial and educational center of the Palouse country with a cornucopia and education personified on its city seal. Courtesy of Washington State University Library.

The cover of a pamphlet advertising North Beach was typical of the colorful brochures of the day. Courtesy of Oregon Historical Society.

Fire!

lthough the Chicago fire of 1871 was probably the most famous of the conflagrations that swept through nineteenth century cities built of wood, it was hardly the only one. Indeed, substantial sections of nearly every American city and small town burned at least once. It is not surprising that one of the first improvements in any town was the installation of a water main for fire protection.

Washington's year of statehood was also a year of fire. On June 6, 1889, an inferno raged through the heart of downtown Seattle and leveled sixty acres, or more than thirty blocks, to cause damages estimated at $10 million. "Every bank, every wholesale house, every hotel, every newspaper office, and nearly every store has been swept out of existence," the *Post-Intelligencer* reported.

On the Fourth of July, Ellensburg burned. In early August, Spokane firemen attending a small blaze could not get their hydrants to work. The resulting fire burned thirty-two blocks and brought down the Howard Street bridge. "A boom of logs took fire and shimmered for hours on the crystal surface of the river, igniting the mammoth lumber and flour mills that line its banks," the *Spokane Falls Review* wrote, celebrating the "heroic efforts" that limited the blaze to the south bank.

In the young cities, the fires served to advance the modernization process. Neighboring towns sent immediate relief, and businesses reopened quickly in tents. Banks loaned money for new stock and for up-to-date buildings made of brick and stone, often several stories high. Labor was in great demand, and the cities spent considerably more on rebuilding than they had lost to the flames.

Photographers documented Seattle's fire almost from the moment it started. This is an early shot of the corner of First and Madison. Courtesy of Special Collections Division, University of Washington Libraries.

A sign advertising safe deposit vaults provides an ironic note in this photograph of the ruins at the corner of First and Cherry in Seattle. Courtesy of Special Collections Division, University of Washington Libraries.

Businesses quickly reopened in the acres of tents, pictured here in Spokane, that arose immediately in the ashes of the 1889 fires in Spokane and Seattle. Courtesy of Eastern Washington State Historical Society.

The fires in larger cities alarmed small town officials and businessmen into installing gravity-fed water systems for fire hoses. This was the official test of the Waitsburg municipal waterworks, about 1890. Courtesy of Special Collections Division, University of Washington Libraries.

The Road to Statehood

As early as 1868, Dakota, Montana, Idaho, Wyoming, and Washington had all been organized as territories, but because they were remote and inaccessible, their populations grew slowly. Not until the completion of the Northern Pacific Railroad in 1883 did rapid peopling of the northern territories make talk of statehood realistic. In 1880 these territories had an aggregate population of 302,851. Ten years and hundreds of miles of railroad track later, the population of what became the so-called "Omnibus States" had swelled to 1,138,166.

In the early 1880s Congress was not disposed to admit any new states. The major stumbling block was the Democratic Party. The admission of Colorado in 1876 gave the Republicans their margin of victory in that year's controversial presidential election. Fearful that Republicans would gain electoral

On November 18, 1889, Elisha P. Ferry took the oath of office as Washington's first state governor on the steps of the old frontier capitol, duly decorated for the occasion. Courtesy of Washington State Capital Museum.

80

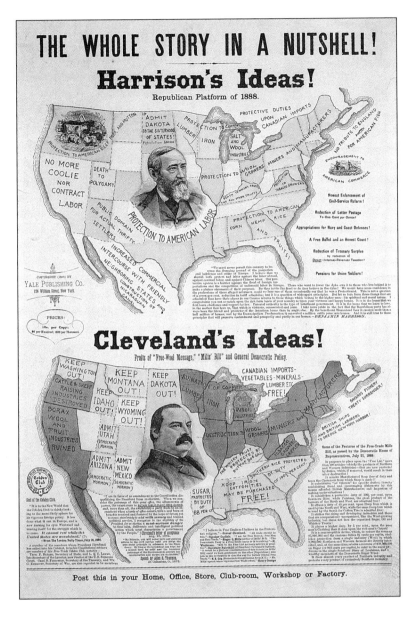

A Republican campaign poster from the election of 1888 reveals the importance of western issues and admission politics.
Courtesy of Chicago Historical Society.

Republican-oriented Dakota (one state) and Washington, Democratically inclined New Mexico, and Montana, a swing state.

Democratic strategy in the lame-duck session was to admit one state favorable to their interests and limit damage by admitting only one Dakota before Republicans gained control of the federal government on March 4, 1889. This was the "Omnibus Bill" (doing several things at once), but the Republican Senate would not pass it, recognizing that time was on their side.

Emerging from a conference committee, the Omnibus Bill carried a Democratic title, but its features were definitely Republican. Also known as the Enabling Act for North and South Dakota, Washington, and Montana, this bill authorized the territories to convene constitutional conventions in their respective capitals on the Fourth of July. It ignored New Mexico, Idaho, and Wyoming. On February 22, 1889, President Cleveland signed the act.

The Washington constitutional convention met in the old territorial capitol building in Olympia. The proposed constitution and an initial slate of candidates for state elected offices were placed before the voters on October 1, along with three separate ballot issues dealing with prohibition, women's suffrage, and the state capital.

The constitution gained voter approval and Olympia emerged as the leading candidate for the seat of government, but the two other measures failed. With the president's approval, Washington became the nation's forty-second state on November 11, 1889.

votes from newly admitted western states, Democrats used their control of the House of Representatives to block several territories from joining the Union. It took the election of 1888, when the Republicans carried both houses of Congress and the presidency, to break the logjam.

In the lame-duck session of Congress held shortly after the election, Democrats bowed to the inevitable. They hoped that by admitting the new states Democrats might win favor in the eyes of new voters. On December 17, 1888, the Democrats in the House Committee on Territories reported a bill calling for the admission of

Washington's Capital Controversies

Washington is one of the few states that has had only one seat of government. But not for lack of alternative sites. Washington's first territorial governor, Isaac Stevens, designated Olympia as the "temporary capital." Due to the honor and economic benefit accruing to a capital city, other struggling settlements of western Washington were envious of Olympia's honored status and fought to have the seat of government moved.

Those early efforts peaked in 1860–61 when the territorial assembly passed a bill relocating the capital to Vancouver. But the legislature approved this measure in such haste—in order to surprise the opposition—that it lacked an enabling clause and date of passage, and in time the Territorial Supreme Court nullified it on that technicality. This preserved Olympia's status until the time of admission.

Population growth in eastern Washington resurrected the issue of Olympia's suitability as capital—particularly its lack of central location. The constitutional convention of 1889 put the matter to voters in a referendum. In a contest that quickly narrowed to Olympia and two central Washington candidates, Ellensburg and Yakima, the incumbent emerged victorious.

The growth of state government required larger quarters, but an attempt to build a new capitol in the 1890s failed. Instead, Populist governor John R. Rogers conceived and implemented a plan to buy Thurston County's recently completed courthouse for office space and add an annex to house the legislative chambers.

Olympia continued to fight off cities, chiefly Tacoma, that coveted the seat of government. Indeed, the first legislature to meet in what is now called the Old Capitol Building (1905) passed a bill calling for another public vote on the location of the

This is the Washington Capitol that might have been; a drawing of the proposed (but never completed) design of architect Ernest Flagg. Courtesy of Washington State Capital Museum.

Washington's current legislative building emerges from a maze of scaffolding, 1926.
Courtesy of Washington State Capital Museum.

capital. Governor Albert Mead vetoed the measure, citing popular weariness with the issue.

Olympia did not become the secure home of state government until completion of the present legislative building in 1927. With a tremendous financial investment in a permanent and prestigious capitol group, it became clear that the public would never seriously consider locating the seat of government elsewhere.

Governor John R. Rogers turns dirt for the construction of a legislative annex to the former Thurston County Courthouse. The contractor, F. H. Goss of Tacoma, is the second from the left; the architect, Willis Ritchie of Spokane, is the fifth from the left.
Courtesy of Washington State Capital Museum.

Washington Counties

	Created by Oregon Provisional Government	
County	Date of Organization	Origin of Place-name
Clark	June 27, 1844	Capt. William Clark
Lewis	December 21, 1845	Capt. Meriwether Lewis
	Created by Oregon Territorial Legislature	
Pacific	February 4, 1851	Ocean boundary
Thurston	January 12, 1852	Oregon's first Congressional Delegate Samuel R. Thurston
Jefferson	December 22, 1852	President Thomas Jefferson
King	December 22, 1852	Vice-president-elect William R. King
Pierce	December 22, 1852	President-elect Franklin Pierce
Island	January 6, 1853	Composed of islands

Olympia was territorial capital and seat of Thurston County in 1879. Courtesy of Library of Congress.

Port Townsend in 1878, now the county seat of Jefferson County. Courtesy of Museum of History and Industry.

Created by Washington Territorial Legislature

County	Date of Organization	Origin of Place-name
Skamania	March 9, 1854	"Swift water"
Whatcom	March 9, 1854	Nooksack chief
Mason*	March 13, 1854	First Territorial Secretary Charles H. Mason
Grays Harbor+	April 14, 1854	Capt. Robert Gray
Cowlitz	April 21, 1854	"Capturing the medicine spirit"
Wahkiakum	April 25, 1854	Chinook chief
Walla Walla	April 25, 1854	"Small rapid river"
Clallam	April 26, 1854	"Big brave nation"
Kitsap#	January 16, 1857	"Brave;" name of Suquamish chief
Spokane	January 29, 1858	"Children of the sun"
Klickitat	December 20, 1859	"Beyond" (mountains) in Chinook language
Snohomish	January 14, 1861	"Union of men" (or warriors)
Stevens	January 20, 1863	Gov. Isaac I. Stevens
Yakima	January 21, 1865	"People of the narrow river"
Whitman	November 29, 1871	Missionary Marcus Whitman
San Juan	October 31, 1873	Archipelago named by Spanish explorers

Continued on next page

* Originally called Sawamish County, renamed on January 3, 1864, after Mason, who had died in 1859.
+ Originally called Chehalis County.
# Originally called Slaughter County after W. A. Slaughter, deceased veteran of Indian War of 1855.

Created by Washington Territorial Legislature (continued)

County	Date of Organization	Origin of Place-name
Columbia	November 11, 1875	Columbia River
Garfield	November 29, 1881	President James A. Garfield
Asotin	October 27, 1883	"Eel creek" in Nez Perce language
Kittitas	November 24, 1883	"Gray gravel bank"
Lincoln	November 24, 1883	President Abraham Lincoln
Adams	November 28, 1883	President John Adams
Douglas	November 28, 1883	Sen. Stephen A. Douglas
Franklin	November 28, 1883	Benjamin Franklin
Skagit	November 28, 1883	Skagit Indian tribe
Okanogan	February 2, 1888	"Rendezvous"

Created by Washington State Legislature

County	Date of Organization	Origin of Place-name
Ferry	February 21, 1899	Gov. Elisha P. Ferry
Chelan	March 13, 1899	"Deep water"
Benton	March 8, 1905	Sen. Thomas Hart Benton
Grant	February 24, 1909	President Ulysses S. Grant
Pend Oreille	March 1, 1911	French term meaning "ear bobs" applied to Indians wearing pendants

Fairhaven in 1891, now a part of Bellingham, seat of Whatcom County. Courtesy of State Historical Society of Wisconsin.

Cheney in 1884, at that time the seat of Spokane County. A short time later it lost that status to the growing city of Spokane. Courtesy of Library of Congress.

Dayton in 1884, the seat of Columbia County. Courtesy of Library of Congress.

The Klondike Rush

After four hard years of depression that began in 1893, Washington needed to regain its economic health. The tonic it sought came in the form of news of the fabulous Klondike bonanza. Word of the gold discovery reached Seattle in July 1897, and seemingly overnight the state was abuzz with talk of fortune and adventure. The Seattle waterfront became a hive of activity as thousands of adventurers set sail for Alaska and the Yukon.

Seattle successfully promoted itself as the gateway to the North. A special Klondike edition of the *Post-Intelligencer* reached the country's seven thousand postmasters, six hundred public libraries, and four thousand mayors. The Great Northern distributed another ten thousand copies and the Northern Pacific six thousand. This public relations feat not only spurred the city's growth but also linked Seattle and Alaska in the public mind for decades to come.

The Klondike Gold Rush stimulated Seattle's economy. These twelve 175-foot Yukon River steamers were built that year by the Moran Brothers Company. Courtesy of Museum of History and Industry.

Gold seekers leave Seattle for the Klondike aboard the SS Willamette. *This was the easy part of the journey. Ahead lay Dyea or Skagway and an arduous overland trek to the Yukon.*
Courtesy of Washington State Historical Society.

Seattle outfitters provisioned the fortune seekers bound for the Klondike in 1898. Courtesy of Washington State Historical Society.

Apple Craze

Between 1905 and 1915 an apple craze gripped eastern Washington. In almost every county "fruit land" was sold to prospective horticulturists, who soon planted it with millions of acres of orchards. Promoters promised that one day even the Palouse would become "the most famous apple country in the United States."

In Spokane, the annual fruit fair changed its name to the Apple Fair in 1908, and a few years later it became the National Apple Show. Its colorful, eye-catching displays contained apples from all over the region, sometimes arranged in the shape of clocks, waterfalls, or oversized apples.

The idyllic promise of minimal labor and constant profit attracted many gentleman and lady farmers. The appeal, as one promotional flier proclaimed, was to "Quit the Strenuous Life" for a life of leisure. "Take care of your trees five years, and they will take care of you the rest of your life." Alas, predictions of the fortunes to be made in apple orchards rarely came true for individuals without farming experience.

The successful grower specialized in limited varieties of apples in order to take advantage of favorable railroad rates for carload lots. Boxes of individually wrapped Winesaps, Delicious, Jonathans, and Romes sold early to a luxury market. The large size and superior appearance of Washington fruit commanded high prices.

But as more and more trees came into production, the resulting market glut changed the apple industry. Some growers abandoned their orchards while others joined cooperative ventures that sold their produce under promoted brand names. Apple production survived in those geographical areas best suited for fruit growing.

Although the craze had run its course

It is not surprising to see rows upon rows of apple trees depicted on the cover of this colorful Wenatchee promotional pamphlet, since the city's growth and development depended on the boom in apple production. Courtesy of Washington State Historical Society.

by 1920, it catapulted Washington to top place in the United States apple industry. Today the irrigated lands of the Yakima, Wenatchee, and Okanogan districts produce the majority of the apples in the state.

This late 1920s apple-picking crew in Spring Valley was a part of the more than thirty-five thousand agricultural workers who picked, graded, and packed the fruit during harvest season. The industry depended on migrant labor. Courtesy of Eastern Washington State Historical Society.

Washington growers, who depended increasingly on a national market, advertised their product widely. This playful postcard announces the arrival of the Third National Apple Show in Chicago. Courtesy of Special Collections Division, University of Washington Libraries.

Women's Suffrage

Posters were only one of many means used by women in their campaign for the vote.
Courtesy of Special Collections Division, University of Washington Libraries.

ashington voters in 1910 approved a state constitutional amendment that gave women the right to vote. That was ten years before passage of the national women's suffrage amendment.

The 1910 victory marked the culmination of a lengthy "votes for women" battle. Twice during territorial days the legislature had granted women the right to vote only to be overruled by the courts. Voters defeated a proposal to include women's suffrage in the new state constitution in 1889. After statehood, trips to Washington by the Oregon suffragist Abigail Scott Duniway and national leader Susan B. Anthony helped revitalize the state's equal rights advocates.

Leaders were divided over the means by which to achieve their goal. In Seattle, paid national organizer Emma Smith

Songs, speeches, and reports filled the two-day program of the 1907 Washington Equal Suffrage Association convention. It was a rejuvenated movement supported by grassroots organizing that helped spread the message throughout the state. Courtesy of Joseph Smith Papers, Manuscripts and University Archives, University of Washington Libraries.

Annual conventions of the Washington Equal Suffrage Association brought together women's rights advocates from all over the state. Delegates to the nineteenth annual meeting in Seattle identified themselves by ribbons, such as this one. Courtesy of Nellie Fick Papers, Manuscripts and University Archives, University of Washington Libraries.

DeVoe led the State Equal Suffrage Association in "essentially a womanly campaign, emphasizing the home interests and engaging the cooperation of home makers." They successfully lobbied the state legislature to include a proposed constitutional amendment on the 1910 ballot.

From Spokane, flamboyant May Arkwright Hutton directed a vigorous campaign as president of the Washington Political Equality League. Among the techniques employed by Hutton's more radical group were public demonstrations, parade floats, stump speeches, and suffrage songs. The efforts of both these organizations along with those of the state Grange, College Women's Suffrage Clubs, and the Women's Christian Temperance Union led Washington's all-male electorate to approve the amendment by an almost two-to-one majority.

Reclamation: Agrarian Dreams and Schemes

With an average annual rainfall as low as six inches in some locations, much of eastern Washington requires irrigation to grow its crops. Over the years, numerous engineering schemes have sought to transform the bunchgrass and sage landscape of the Columbia Plateau into a new Garden of Eden.

> Nowhere in the wide west has there been more consistent and intelligent exploitation of irrigation than in Yakima Valley. The reason for this is in the perfect conditions of water, soil, and climate (supplied by a beneficent Providence), and the application of brains, common sense, and scientific methods of farming.

The Yakima Valley, as promoted in this quotation from the Northern Pacific Railway in 1911, became a showplace of irrigated agriculture.

As was also true in the Wenatchee and Okanogan valleys, the earliest efforts to irrigate the Yakima Valley began with individual or community projects to divert streams into nearby fields. Private companies soon invested in the construction of canals, such as the Sunnyside Canal between Yakima and Prosser, and laid plans to create massive storage reservoirs. The towns of the valley sought to create "an advanced type" of community that blended the best elements of rural and urban life.

When Congress passed the Newlands Reclamation Act in 1902, the federal government became directly involved in irrigation projects. One of the first acts of the United States Reclamation Service was to take over the Sunnyside Project, which by 1905 was providing homes for

"IRRIGATION IN THE UNITED STATES MEANS AN EMPIRE OF ONE MILLION SQUARE MILES WHICH WILL SUPPORT 200,000,000 PEOPLE."

"The Beautiful Sunnyside Valley," the site of the state's first United States Reclamation Project, was promoted as a future garden paradise. Courtesy of Washington State Historical Society.

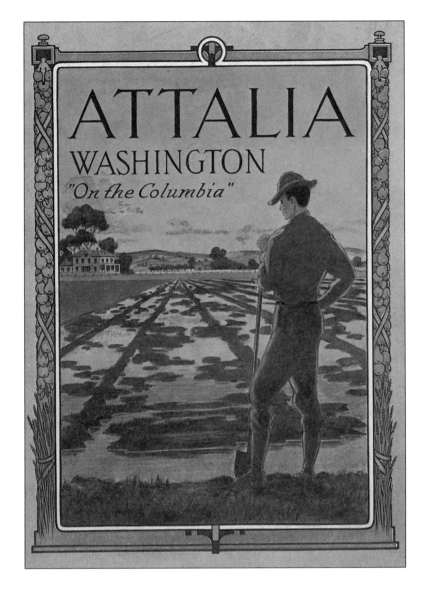

A brochure promoting Attalia in western Walla Walla County idealized life on the irrigation frontier. Courtesy of Oregon Historical Society.

The National Irrigation Congress worked for the reclamation of arid and semiarid land throughout the West. Their seventeenth annual meeting in Spokane, advertised by this Great Northern Railway brochure, included tours of the state's famous irrigation districts. Courtesy of Minnesota Historical Society.

five thousand people. The Reclamation Service settled questions of conflicting water rights and established the Tieton, Okanogan, and other irrigation programs. Federal involvement also stimulated activity by private companies in the Yakima Valley, where 334,440 acres had been irrigated by 1911.

According to the Great Northern Railway:

> The story of what irrigation has accomplished in Washington reads like a chapter from the tales of the *Arabian Nights*. Its reality even transcends any imaginative thing narrated in those old tales.

Nonetheless, when those words were written in 1909, the amount of land under irrigation was still a small percentage of the state's total farmland. Although New Deal projects in the 1930s would pursue similar dreams and irrigated lands would continue to be developed, the rhetoric of reclamation in Washington almost always outstripped its realities.

The Wobblies

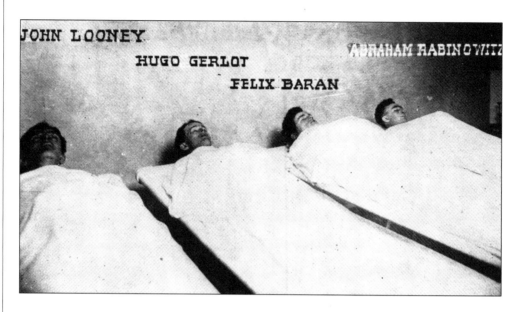

IWW supporters printed this extraordinary postcard as a fund raiser. Above the space for correspondence, the reverse reads, "DIED FOR FREE SPEECH — THE EVERETT MASSACRE — Bloody Sunday, November 5, 1916 — Send help to: Box 1878, Seattle, Washington." Courtesy of Special Collections Division, University of Washington Libraries.

The Industrial Workers of the World was formed in Chicago in 1905 and remained strong in Washington until the start of the First World War. The IWW, or Wobblies, organized along class lines to eliminate the divisions that separated workers in one craft or trade from those in others. "An Injury to One is the Concern of All," the Wobblies declared, and "The Working Class and the Employing Class Have Nothing In Common."

Colorful, committed, spirited, and proud despite vigilant attacks and jail sentences, the IWW appealed to people enduring the poor working and living conditions on the Northwest wageworkers' frontier. Eight hundred people joined the IWW in Seattle in 1905, and locals were established in Tacoma and Bellingham within the next year. Wobbly organizers came to Aberdeen and Hoquiam in 1912, marching from mill to mill in an effort to persuade workers to leave their jobs.

In Spokane, the IWW claimed four thousand members, had a meeting hall seating eight hundred, and after 1909,

The stacked bed rolls of migratory harvest hands in the Palouse country. Many workers packed everything they owned in their bed rolls. Courtesy of Idaho Historical Society.

Although they posed for photographers brandishing their banners and their publications, Wobblies entertained themselves like members of other early twentieth century organizations at family functions like this picnic, held in Seattle during July 1919. Courtesy of Special Collections Division, University of Washington Libraries.

published a newspaper, the *Industrial Worker*. Organizers stood on boxes to give speeches to the migrant workers for whom the city served as a hiring center for jobs in the nearby forests, mines, and fields. In 1909 city officials outlawed such public speaking and arrested IWW speakers, although they did not interfere with street-corner preachers.

As IWW speakers were arrested in Spokane, more came from all over the country, filling the jails and an abandoned schoolhouse that served as an overflow facility. Publicized across the nation, the Spokane Free Speech Fight ended when

Wobblies overburdened Spokane's jail facilities and its treasury, and city officials revoked the licenses of nineteen employment agencies that IWW activists had accused of dishonest practices.

In 1916 the IWW attempted to use the free speech tactic in a shingle weavers' strike in Everett. On one occasion citizen-deputies mobilized by the sheriff against the IWW took forty Wobblies into a wooded park and beat and whipped them.

On November 5, about 250 Seattle Wobblies on a small chartered ship were met in Everett by several hundred armed men, including the sheriff. Someone fired a shot, and soon five Wobblies and two townspeople were dead, with fifty wounded and an unknown number drowned. Seventy-four IWW members were arrested for murder; one was acquitted and the charges against the rest were dropped. No charges were filed against the sheriff and his men. The Everett Massacre was the bloodiest single episode of labor-related violence in Washington history.

A Radical Heritage

Dr. Hermon F. Titus, a Harvard-educated physician, became a leader in Seattle's radical community in the early twentieth century. In this 1912 publication he advocated the implementation of a four-hour workday by 1920. Courtesy of Manuscripts and University Archives, University of Washington Libraries.

James Farley, Postmaster General of the United States and confidant of President Franklin D. Roosevelt, is supposed to have offered a toast in the mid 1930s to "the forty-seven states in the Union, and the Soviet of Washington." His oft-quoted remark probably referred to the Washington Commonwealth Federation and a host of new and sometimes bizarre reform programs that enlivened political debate in the Evergreen State during the Depression decade.

In many ways what Farley observed was only the latest manifestation of a Washington tradition already several decades old. Thirty years earlier, a far less prominent figure observed that Washington was home to "more 'isms' and 'osophies' than any other state in America."

Washington's radical heritage took several forms. One was a vigorous socialist movement in the early years of the twentieth century. Another was left-wing unionism in the guise of the Industrial Workers of the World. A third was a series of utopian socialist and anarchist colonies.

Distressed by the shortcomings of the new industrial society, a group of Washingtonians founded the Puget Sound Co-Operative Colony near Port Angeles in the mid 1880s. This was the first of several utopian experiments on Puget Sound that attracted builders of a brave new world to a remote but promising corner of the globe.

Utopian colonies such as Home, Equality, and Freeland arose on the sound's isolated bays and tidal flats. Many

At Equality Colony, one of several utopian settlements on Puget Sound in the 1890s, members of the Brotherhood of the Cooperative Commonwealth urged people to read their newspaper, Industrial Freedom. Courtesy of Special Collections Division, University of Washington Libraries.

members dreamed of transforming Washington into a model commonwealth, a workable alternative to the larger industrial society that seemed to suffer more social tension and economic dislocation with each passing year. No less a figure than John R. Rogers, Washington's Populist governor from 1897 to 1901, encouraged visionaries who believed the young state offered the most opportunities and fewest obstacles to overcome in their quest for utopia.

The Socialists of Seattle advertised a picnic to all interested people. In the opening decade of the twentieth century, the party in Washington claimed to have the highest per capita membership in the nation. The party's political fortunes peaked in the 1912 election, when 12 percent of the state's electorate voted Socialist. Photograph by Asahel Curtis courtesy of Washington State Historical Society.

Urban Magnets

Washington's population in 1910 was forty-seven times larger than it had been in 1870, though the state still had barely a million residents. More than half of them lived in communities of twenty-five hundred or more people, places the federal census defined as urban. Although the state in 1910 was more urban than the United States as a whole, few Washington towns included more than ten thousand residents, and only Seattle, Spokane, and Tacoma could be called cities.

Ray Stannard Baker, a prominent national journalist, observed in 1903 that in the Pacific Northwest "everything seems to have happened within the last ten years." And in many ways it had. The cities of Seattle, Tacoma, and Spokane experienced spectacular growth after the turn of the century, when all three spent millions of dollars on new public buildings and developed modern downtown areas.

No city in Washington grew faster than Spokane. In 1880 it was a village of 350 people. During the next decade the Northern Pacific Railroad connected Spokane to the rest of the world and to the booming mining regions in eastern Washington and nearby Idaho. Spokane's population reached 20,000 in 1890 and topped 100,000 by 1910.

Seattle grew in population and size as it incorporated towns that had once been suburbs. First the city extended north by annexing Green Lake and the area beyond the University of Washington. During the

This aerial view of Spokane shows how the city clusters around the falls of the Spokane River. The demolition that preceeded the city's 1974 world's fair removed the railroad tracks from Havermale Island and along the river. The Monroe Street Bridge is in the foreground. Courtesy of Eastern Washington State Historical Society.

The expanding metropolis encompassed residential sections for people of all classes, as well as the growing downtowns. This Seattle neighborhood was photographed in 1927.
Courtesy of Library of Congress.

first decade of the twentieth century, Seattle more than doubled its area when it annexed the suburbs of Ballard, West Seattle, and Rainier Beach. In new parts of town, as in older ones, developers bought tracts of land and erected rows or

blocks of nearly identical houses. Meanwhile, as speculators rushed to acquire downtown land, values increased by as much as 25 percent a year.

For years the most notable structure in the state was Seattle's L. C. Smith

Looking south along Walla Walla's main street in 1923. The city has managed to preserve many of its downtown structures to the present time. Photograph by Wesley Andrews courtesy of Oregon Historical Society.

Building, designed by a firm from Syracuse, New York, and completed in 1913. At forty-two stories, the Smith Tower, as it came to be known, was for many years the tallest building west of the Mississippi River.

In Seattle, Tacoma, and Spokane, as in much smaller towns and villages, development required public services. As population density increased, water and sewage systems and provisions for the removal of garbage became matters of good public health.

Port commissions issued bonds to finance improvements. They erected piers, warehouses, and grain elevators to make their ports attractive to commerce. The Port of Seattle, an independent agency established in 1911, created a special pier for lumber at Smith Cove, the Salmon Bay terminal moorage for the fishing fleet, and nearly thirty city blocks of open wharf space.

Smaller towns graded and paved their streets to attract commerce and to accommodate the automobiles that came to town on newly built roads. Stores lined their developing main streets, equipped in some cases with modern utilities like the streets of the big cities.

In 1914, the year after completion of the tallest building in the Pacific Northwest, Asahel Curtis juxtaposed Seattle's forty-two story Smith Tower with the region's highest natural landmark, Mount Rainier. Courtesy of Oregon Historical Society.

Automobiles lined the main street of Colfax, the Whitman County seat, in the 1920s.
Courtesy of Washington State University Library.

Picnickers and cows witness the arrival of the Great White Fleet in Tacoma, 1908. Sixteen American battle ships were sailing around the world, visiting every continent in a demonstration of—and public relations tour for—President Theodore Roosevelt's "big stick" policies. Courtesy of Library of Congress.

Horses, streetcars, automobiles, and pedestrians share the streets of downtown Spokane in this turn-of-the-century view. Courtesy of Oregon Historical Society.

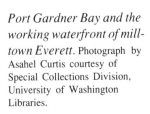

Port Gardner Bay and the working waterfront of milltown Everett. Photograph by Asahel Curtis courtesy of Special Collections Division, University of Washington Libraries.

Stores and Shopping

 erchants held prominent positions in the aspiring towns and cities. Small-town people depended on the general store, city folk on the neighborhood grocery.

The big city department stores all started early. Spokane's Crescent, originally housed in the only building to survive the great fire of 1889, later moved to larger quarters a few blocks east. In Seattle, the Bon Marche, Frederick and Nelson, and Wallin and Nordstrom's shoe store all expanded during the twentieth century.

Seattle's Pike Place Market opened in 1907 when the city established a free market where farmers could sell directly to customers. Covered stalls were added during the next ten years. The Sanitary Market was built in 1910, and the Corner

Jim Kyes' Monte Cristo store, shown here in 1902, sold produce, patent medicines, and a variety of nationally advertised canned goods. Kyes is the mustached man to the right. Courtesy of Special Collections Division, University of Washington Libraries.

Market Building in 1912.

By 1927 more than four hundred farmers sold produce at the Pike Place Market at the height of the growing season. But their numbers declined during the Second World War, and the market deteriorated. After a long campaign, Seattle voters passed an initiative in 1971 designed to restore and protect the traditional character of the market and to establish a seven-acre historic district administered by a citizens' commission.

Grocery departments in the downtown stores used marketing techniques unavailable to neighborhood merchants, such as this promotional tie-in of waffle irons and flour at Seattle's Bon Marche, about 1920. Department stores employed decorators who incorporated the pyramids of products common at small groceries into compelling displays using mirrors, mannequins, and effective lighting. Courtesy of Special Collections Division, University of Washington Libraries.

The Pike Place Market, shown here in a 1912 Asahel Curtis photograph, was the major regional expression of a national movement to eliminate middlemen and bring producers and consumers into direct contact. Courtesy of Special Collections Division, University of Washington Libraries.

Public Transportation

Beginning in 1884 with the founding of the Seattle Street Railway, Seattle and eventually several smaller cities were served by a variety of street railways powered by horses, cables, and electricity. After 1900 most of the Seattle companies consolidated as part of the Boston-owned Seattle Electric Company, and eventually merged into the Puget Sound Traction, Light and Power Company. In 1912, the city government established the Seattle Municipal Railway to construct new lines and to buy out the private interests.

Streetcars ran between cities as well as within them. Electric interurban lines ran from Spokane to Coeur d'Alene and Moscow, Idaho, and from Seattle to Tacoma and Everett, and linked various communities in the Walla Walla and Yakima valleys. After the First World War, automobile traffic increased. By the Great Depression most of the electric interurbans had quit hauling passengers and some lines were abandoned entirely.

With the coming of better roads and gasoline-powered vehicles, motor busses became a feature of public transportation. In a state long dominated by water transportation, ferryboats carried foot passengers, horses, wagons, and eventually automobiles. Long before statehood, ferries operated on the Columbia River. Their early regulation by the legislature perhaps foreshadowed the state-run ferry system on Puget Sound in later years.

The cable car from Lake Washington to the bottom of Madison Street passes the Third Avenue Theatre in this Asahel Curtis photograph taken in early 1907, the year the once-popular theater was torn down.
Courtesy of Special Collections Division, University of Washington Libraries.

Public transportation made outings possible in smaller towns, where entrepreneurs established services like the Grays Harbor Automobile and Omnibus Company. Courtesy of Special Collections Division, University of Washington Libraries.

The "Shoshone Flyer" was a part of the electric interurban system that linked many small towns of the Inland Northwest to Spokane. Courtesy of Washington State Historical Society.

The ferry docked at the Bellevue landing in 1914. A quarter of a century later the small town's population was still a little over a thousand, and a guidebook described it as "a trading center for the berry farmers and vineyardists in the rich lowlands." Courtesy of Special Collections Division, University of Washington Libraries.

Engineering a New Washington

The story of Seattle's regrades is so unusual that it has overshadowed the many other ways Washingtonians altered the natural boundaries of the land they settled. Often using the most up-to-date engineering, they blasted tunnels, built bridges, and revamped rivers and harbors to overcome the state's formidable natural barriers.

The idea for a canal linking Puget Sound with Seattle's two main lakes was first suggested at a meeting of the city's pioneers. Thomas Mercer proposed

The ship canal linking Lake Washington to Puget Sound, first proposed by Seattle's pioneers, was completed by the Army Corps of Engineers in 1916. The capacity of those locks was exceeded in America at that time only by those of the Panama Canal.
Courtesy of Library of Congress.

calling the smaller of the two "Lake Union" in the understanding that it would someday merit the name. The Lake Washington Canal Company was incorporated in 1871, and fifteen years later it had completed a small canal in which logs could be floated between the lakes. Eventually the federal government took over the rights-of-way, and the Army Corps of Engineers completed the task, in part with money raised by a special property levy in King County. The Lake Washington Ship Canal opened in 1916.

The Army Corps did considerable dredging and other work on Washington rivers and harbors. By 1902 it had undertaken projects intended to improve navigation on the Willapa, Cowlitz, Okanogan, and Pend Oreille rivers, and into the harbors at Everett and Olympia—eighteen projects in all, totaling nearly $12 million, including projects shared with Oregon on the Columbia and

The Tacoma Narrows Bridge, unstable and dubbed "Galloping Gertie" from the time it opened in 1940, is shown here in midcollapse. Courtesy of Farquharson Collection, University of Washington Libraries.

The Denny Regrade

Mayors, council members, and planning commissioners would hate to admit it, but the municipal officers who often leave the most lasting legacies are city engineers. Certainly that was true in the case of R. H. Thomson and the city of Seattle. He was the man who reshaped the natural landscape to fit his image of urbanity.

Thomson became Seattle's city engineer in 1892. A proponent of municipal water supplies, he later challenged private power interests by making Seattle one of the first major cities in the nation to generate and distribute its own hydroelectric power.

The last and most enduringly visible of Thomson's great civic missions was to dig Seattle out of what he perceived to be a pit bounded on three sides by hills that hampered the city's prospects for development.

Between 1902 and 1910, Thomson sluiced Denny Hill north of the downtown area into Elliott Bay. The sculpting power of water pumped from Lake Union to the top of the hill undermined homes and business establishments on the old natural landscape. For a while, many buildings towered precariously above the new, flat, more valuable street frontage of what has come to be known as the "Regrade."

Ironically, as downtown Seattle moved gradually north after the fire of 1889, it failed to utilize the regraded land in any significant way until the post–Second World War urban boom. Still, Thomson's regrade demonstrated the power of modern engineering to reshape the region's landscape and political economy.

The vicinity of Fourth and Bell streets in Seattle gets resculptured.
Courtesy of Special Collections Division, University of Washington Libraries.

This tunnel through the Cascades from Scenic to Berne was completed in 1929. It was considered an engineering marvel, the longest railway tunnel in the Americas. Courtesy of Eastern Washington State Historical Society.

DIAGRAM OF THE GREAT EIGHT-MILE LONG CASCADE TUNNEL WASHINGTON. NOTE THE OLD TUNNEL HIGH ABOVE THE PRESENT TUNNEL COMPLETED IN 1929

Snake rivers.

The Monroe Street Bridge in Spokane was another major engineering accomplishment. When completed in 1911, its 281-foot-long reinforced concrete arch was the world's longest.

The first Tacoma Narrows Bridge, spanning Puget Sound at its narrowest point, was less successful. A creation of the firm that planned both San Francisco's Golden Gate and New York's George Washington bridges, it was described by the head of that firm as the "most beautiful in the world." The bridge rippled from the time it opened in 1940, and earned the nickname "Galloping Gertie." It collapsed four months later, with no human fatalities.

The cumulative effects of water's erosive power, manipulated by urban engineers, created this surrealistic scene captured by Asahel Curtis. Courtesy of Special Collections Division, University of Washington Libraries.

Communities by Design

In a sparsely settled state where extractive industries flourished, many companies built not only work places, but also employee houses and stores. In wilderness environments milling and mining interests erected company towns where married workers and their families lived in company housing, shopped in company stores, sent their children to company schools, and depended on the fortunes of the company as their own.

In 1853 the firm of Pope and Talbot built Port Gamble, a town that featured a tree-lined main street, fine housing for executives, and a community hall. Workers lived in rows of small houses, and later in barracks, cottages, and apartment houses. Improvements during the 1920s included a school, a hospital, and a service station.

Kirkland also began as a company town. Its streets were laid out to support the development of a proposed steel mill, but the project failed during the depression of 1893. Before the Second World War, DuPont constructed homes

Rows of identical houses line the Port Blakely waterfront where lumber schooners loaded masts and spars. At one time the mill here was the largest in the world and employed twelve hundred men. Courtesy of Washington State University Library.

The Washington Union Coal Company's town of Tono in 1909. Courtesy of Special Collections Division, University of Washington Libraries.

for approximately 225 employees who manufactured high explosives in a town by the same name near Tacoma.

Other companies sponsored housing projects within established towns, while some enlightened industrialists promoted diversified developments that encouraged competing industry within a "company" town. Lumber baron R. A. Long founded Longview as the first planned city in the Pacific Northwest in 1920, laying out the streets for residential and commercial districts and constructing public parks and buildings. By 1933 eighteen manufacturing establishments operated in Longview, including Long's own sawmill and Weyerhaeuser's huge plant, but building restrictions made the houses expensive for most workers.

One of many brochures that promoted the new community of Longview. Courtesy of Washington State Historical Society.

The Quality of Urban Life

One of Children's Public Playgrounds, Seattle, Wash

Photo by F. H. Nowell.

For the children of the working class, Seattle maintained five public playgrounds, including this one in Lincoln Playground, photographed by F. H. Nowell in 1907.
Courtesy of Museum of History and Industry.

 ost Washington communities were not company towns, nor did they desire to be, but all were aware of the need for at least informal planning to bring order to the urban environment. Individuals worked together to improve the quality of urban life.

Citizens' organizations fostered improvements in everything from public transportation to mail service, libraries, and parks. "All over that state," noted one observer in 1905, "women's clubs have had an uplifting influence upon their surroundings." In Yakima, a circulating library association raised money for a permanent library with "teas, talks, a quartette concert, and a musical."

In Seattle, Spokane, and other late nineteenth century cities, the pressures of rapid population growth made the need for civic improvements obvious. During the Progressive era of the early twentieth century, moral reformers attacked political corruption, "gambling and the social evil (prostitution)." Temperance societies campaigned against liquor sales.

Organizations such as the Young Men's Christian Association and the Young Women's Christian Association sponsored athletic and social activities along with vocational training for city youth. Frequently these reformers were affiliated with religious groups such as the Methodist Episcopal Church, which organized the Tacoma Seamen's Friend Society in 1883.

CALL FOR A

MASS MEETING!

TACOMA
SEAMEN'S FRIEND SOCIETY
TO BE ORGANIZED

WEDNESDAY EVENING, MAY 23d,

The benevolent of all classes are cordially invited to meet in the

Methodist Episcopal Church,

In New Tacoma, on this Wednesday, at 7:45 P. M., to organize a Seamen's Friend Society, for the two Tacomas, auxiliary to the American Seamen's Friend Society of New York.

Rev. J. F. DeVore,   Gen. J. W. Sprague,
Rev. T. C. Armstrong,   A. J. Baker,
Rev. Jos. Beven,   D. D. Clarke,
Rev. H. S. Bonnell,   Rev. G. Atkinson,
Rev. E. C. Oakley,   G. F. Orchard,
          H. A. Littlejohn.

A statement of the objects of this organization will will be made by

CHAPLAIN STUBBS,

Of the American Seamen's Friend Society.

LEDGER JOB PRINT, NEW TACOMA.

The Young Men's Christian Association, which provided this public library in Firdale, was one of the many organizations striving to improve the quality of urban life. Courtesy of Special Collections Division, University of Washington Libraries.

The Tacoma Seamen's Friend Society offered a portside haven for the thousands of sailors who entered Puget Sound every year. This 1883 poster announced the society's first organizational meeting, run by Reverend Robert Stubbs. Courtesy of Washington State Historical Society.

The Spirit of Association

Asahel Curtis photographed this group of early Washington pioneers celebrating at one of their annual meetings. Courtesy of Special Collections Division, University of Washington Libraries.

Washingtonians have long organized themselves into groups of like interest. Perhaps the earliest American club organized within the boundaries of the future state was the Columbia Maternal Association. It was formed in 1838 by Narcissa Whitman and five other Protestant missionary women "for the purpose of adopting such (methods) as are best calculated to assist us in the right performance of our Maternal duties." The group, separated by days of travel, rarely managed to get together in person, but they set aside every second and last Wednesday of the month as days during which to think of each other and their shared duties.

The Columbia Maternal Association was typical of the many small clubs, societies, leagues, organizations,

associations and fellowships that proliferated in the state. In rural areas those institutions worked to bring people together for socializing and sharing common interests, as well as for the discussion of political and economic concerns. A young person on a remote Endicott farm, for example, might belong to a variety of organizations including a debating society, a theatrical group, and regional political organizations.

Local branches of national organizations linked state residents to those in other parts of the country. Members of the Washington State Grange

Catholic cathedrals, Buddhist temples, Jewish synagogues, Quaker meeting houses, revival tents, and Protestant churches are among the structures that testify to the diversity of religions long practiced in the state. As this 1909 communion class indicates, religious practices played an important role in the development of many Washington communities. Courtesy of Special Collections Division, University of Washington Libraries.

joined their voices with farmers nationwide to express their grievances against banks and railroads. During the nineteenth century the Grange, also known as the Patrons of Husbandry, established cooperative organizations and lobbied legislatures to combat high freight and interest rates. Even after the decline of its national political power, the Grange continued to play an important role at the local level in the political and social life of rural communities.

The Delrio Grange No. 828 served as the center of social and business activities for its Big Bend community. Established during the 1920s, the thirty-six-member group met in the rooms above the town store and post office. Every other Saturday night families gathered to shop, pick up mail, and gossip, then they climbed the stairs for the Grange meeting.

Even non-Grange members congregated in the store owner's home to await the ending of the meeting and the beginning of the social hour. The Delrio Grange successfully campaigned for a number of local improvements—better roads, mail service, reliable telephone systems, and rural electrification. They established other community organizations, including a Juvenile Grange, and by 1946 had raised enough money for their own Grange hall.

In urban areas, clubs and associations played a role similar to that of the Grange and other rural organizations. Late nineteenth century women's clubs were typically involved in various types of civic improvement. The Walla Walla Woman's Club, whose members listed the "mutual interchange of ideas" and "self improvement" among their goals, supported women's suffrage.

Elementary and Secondary Education

Washington's first public school was founded in Washougal in 1852, when the future state was still part of Oregon Territory. Two years later the new Washington legislature authorized local public schools. By 1872 the Washington Territory had provided for a superintendent of schools, Washington teachers had held a convention, and students were attending 144 different public schools.

Six high schools opened within a year of statehood, and by the turn of the century, Washington distinguished itself in support of education. The "Barefoot Schoolboy" Law of 1895 provided state support for local school districts, financed by a direct state tax—particularly helpful in rural areas. At first the state supported only common schools, but in the late 1890s it extended support to high schools as well. Beginning in 1888, Washington provided education for handicapped children at the "School for Defective Youth" in Vancouver, which eventually became the state school for the deaf and blind.

To do the work of education properly, University of Washington history professor Edmond Meany exulted in 1909, "Washington pays out money freely and with the most cheerful spirit whenever a call comes from the schools." Indeed, the state led the nation in school money expended per capita. As a result, it ranked among the top three states in literacy, with only 1 percent of the population unable to read and write.

Some schools like this one, photographed in Burbank in 1904, provided the name for the Barefoot Schoolboy Law, which supported local school districts and gave educational opportunities to rural children. Courtesy of Washington State Historical Society.

This building was originally designed as the Tacoma Land Company Hotel, but its construction was suspended during the depression of 1893. It was completed in 1906 as Tacoma's Stadium High School and photographed in this idealized panorama about 1910. Courtesy of Library of Congress.

Washington's progressive program of state support for local education made possible such modern facilities as these at the Anacortes High School in 1904. Courtesy of Special Collections Division, University of Washington Libraries.

Colleges and Universities

Walla Walla's Whitman College, shown here in this 1913 postcard, was the oldest and for some time the largest of the state's private colleges. Courtesy of Special Collections Division, University of Washington Libraries.

T he Washington legislature first attempted to create a university in 1855, but was unsuccessful until 1861, when Arthur Denny, Charles Terry, and Edward Lander gave the state ten acres for a campus, in what would eventually become downtown Seattle. The University of Washington moved to its present location at the end of the century, but it retained the original tract, which by then had substantial commercial value and still continues to provide income to the university. By 1914 the university had thirty-three hundred students and two hundred faculty, and offered teacher training and courses in forestry, engineering, law, and classical subjects.

Soon after statehood, Washington received federal land grant money that had been unavailable to it as a territory, and established "the Washington Agricultural College, Experiment Station and School of Science" at Pullman. The college opened in 1892, with a faculty of

University of Washington women students perform an annual event, a May Fete, in 1920. Courtesy of Special Collections Division, University of Washington Libraries.

five and a student body of sixty. In 1905 the name was changed to the State College of Washington and later to Washington State University. By 1910 a

Men and women students work in Professor Horace Byers's chemistry class at the University of Washington in 1905. Perhaps the sale of the horehound drops suggests less-than-perfect ventilation in the lab.
Webster-Stevens photograph courtesy of Museum of History and Industry.

student body of one thousand studied agriculture, home economics, engineering, and general liberal arts.

The state also operated three "normal schools"—institutions for teacher training—at Cheney, Ellensburg, and Bellingham. Tuition at those schools, as at the university and the state college, was free to all Washington citizens.

Walla Walla's Whitman College, which began holding classes in 1865, was the largest of the state's early private schools, offering one hundred students instruction in classical subjects. The Jesuits established Gonzaga University in 1881 and Seattle University in 1892. Methodists, Presbyterians, Lutherans, and Seventh-Day Adventists also founded small academies that developed into colleges or universities.

After a seventy-five-year lapse in public support for new institutions of higher learning, The Evergreen State College was approved by the legislature in 1967; students first arrived on campus in 1971. Eight junior colleges were in operation on both sides of the Cascades before the

These women were studying home economics, one of the subjects emphasized at land grant colleges, at the state college in Pullman. Courtesy of Washington State University Library.

Second World War. During the late 1960s the state's two-year college system began a considerable expansion, and today twenty-seven community colleges bring postsecondary education to people across Washington.

The Press

Modern Washingtonians, who read newspapers as one kind of news source among many, must stretch their imaginations to understand the importance of the press during much of the state's history. Beginning in 1852 with *The Columbian,* the first paper north of the Columbia River, newspapers served to connect settlers in frontier communities with each other and with the major events of their times. Unlike many midcentury papers, *The Columbian,* published in Olympia every Saturday, was "neutral in politics," meaning that it was not the organ of a particular political party or religious group. For its first few years, it was the only newspaper in Washington Territory, but during the following decades, enterprising Washingtonians founded many other papers. In Olympia alone, six newspapers and one magazine started between 1863 and 1870.

Few of these papers lasted long. Until the turn of the century, most were the production of an individual editor, who might begin with insufficient capital or fail to attract a steady readership. Often working with no staff at all, these editors wrote copy, set type, delivered papers, oversaw billing, and sold advertising. Those who succeeded earned central positions in their communities. Their highly personal journals reflected their own tastes, politics, and ambitions; editorial columns revealed their opinions, often delivered in what came to be known as the "Oregon style"—graphic, torrid, and potentially libelous.

Early day papers were thick with print, carrying no illustrations or cartoons. Advertising was generally confined to the back pages, and simply listed commodities received by local stores. Toward the end of the century, Washington newspapers began to carry national advertising, especially from patent medicine companies, which bought space from

Successful ethnic newspapers could afford up-to-date equipment such as the Merganthaler Linotype machine at the Swedish Tribune, *shown here in 1906.* Courtesy of Museum of History and Industry.

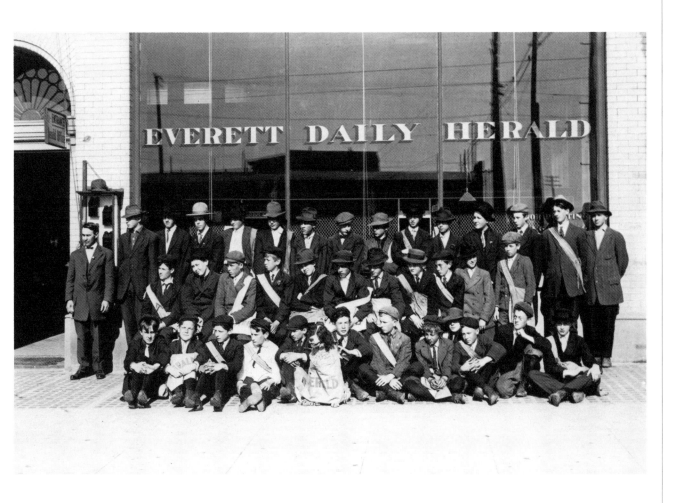

EVERETT DAILY HERALD

Early twentieth century newspaper distribution depended on the children and adolescents who made their living on the streets. Courtesy of Special Collections Division, University of Washington Libraries.

agencies that brokered ads in papers all over the country. National advertising was only one aspect of the major changes that brought the state's papers into the urban-industrial twentieth century.

By 1900 Washington boasted 19 daily and 176 weekly papers. Especially in the larger cities, they reflected less the personal opinions of the editor than the interests of the large businesses they had become. They subscribed to the Associated Press and United Press services, and new technology permitted illustrations. Concentrating on features, crime reporting, and sensationalism, they imitated the new mass papers that William Randolph Hearst and Joseph Pulitzer were making popular throughout the United States.

In Seattle, where a large population supported five daily papers and where radical opinion flourished, newspapers represented a range of political beliefs. The Seattle *Star,* at one time the largest-selling paper in the city, competed with

the more conservative papers by offering a progressive, class-conscious editorial policy and features from the Scripps-Howard chain. The *Union Record,* which began as a weekly, became the only American daily labor newspaper during the First World War, and had a large circulation for many years before it finally went out of business in 1926.

The state has had an active ethnic press as well. Spokane had its *Svenska Pressen,* Tacoma its Norwegian *Western Viking.* South Bend's *Willapa Harbor Pilot,* founded in 1890, published editions in six languages. As late as 1938, Seattle publishers put out Italian, Japanese, black, Jewish, Swedish, German, and Norwegian-Danish papers.

The Performing Arts

F ine arts and literature," wrote University of Washington historian Edmond Meany in his 1909 history of the state, "are never brought to fruition very early in a new community, especially where that community is confronted by the absorbing problems of wild forests, new fields, and mountains of hidden wealth." Meany found some public statuary to praise, and commented on Edward S. Curtis's North American Indian photographs, but the performing arts in the new state were for the most part deemed beneath the notice of refined and cultivated people.

Commercially successful performing art is said to have begun in Seattle with the Theatre Comique, which opened in 1876 in the basement of a Washington Street saloon; Spokane's first variety house raised its curtain ten years later. The shows at those theaters, produced primarily for the many single male wageworkers with time on their hands and some money to spend, featured provocatively dressed women doing song and dance routines.

Eventually the vaudeville circuits consolidated a variety of traveling acts—music and dance, melodramatic skits, acrobats and gymnasts, short films, and other performance art—in non-drinking environments. John Considine built his People's Theater in Spokane into the first popularly priced "polite" circuit. The show cost ten cents. He sold the whole operation in 1913 for $4 million. Alexander Pantages, a Greek immigrant, came to Seattle from Alaska, where he had operated dance halls during the Gold Rush. Beginning in 1902 with his Crystal Theater, he added shows and theaters along the West Coast and by 1915 in the East as well.

Above all, however, Washingtonians relied on themselves for amusement well into the 1920s, when the movies provided frequent diversion for nearly everybody. They competed in roping contests at county fairs, organized amateur symphony orchestras and choral societies, or performed at vaudeville houses on Amateur Night. Women played pianos; men went to band practice and marched in parades on Decoration Day and the Fourth of July. In logging camps and on fishing boats, they told jokes, sang, and played their own musical instruments.

This Tacoma theater shared a name—and a reputation—with Seattle's Theatre Comique, a rowdy "box house" saloon with a theater attached. Courtesy of Special Collections Division, University of Washington Libraries.

Brass bands such as the La Conner Silver Cornet Band, here posing for a group portrait in 1902 at Wingren's Photo Studio in their home town, provided entertainment in small towns all over turn-of-the-century America. Courtesy of Special Collections Division, University of Washington Libraries.

The Third Avenue Theatre, at the corner of Third and Madison in Seattle, at one time had a thousand seats, with one "polite" stage and another for bawdier farce and melodrama. It was torn down in 1907. Courtesy of Special Collections Division, University of Washington Libraries.

III: The Modern Era

*Famed as the longest
concrete pontoon
bridge in the world
(6,661 feet), the Lacey
V. Murrow floating
bridge, shown here on
opening day in 1939,
spurred suburban
development on Mercer
Island and along the
east side of Lake
Washington. A second
and longer
(7,518 feet) floating
bridge across the lake
opened in 1962 and
furthered the
suburbanization of
metropolitan Seattle.*
Courtesy of Special
Collections Division,
University of Washington
Libraries.

127

Two key events in the modern era of Washington's history were the world wars. Both meant a combination of regimentation, optimism, sorrow, and prosperity. Before each conflict, the state's economy had been in a slump. But the wars made jobs plentiful. Women entered the work force as never before, although in most cases their employment was only temporary. More than anything else, the world wars propelled the state toward maturity.

The draft, enacted in 1917, symbolized the changes the First World War brought to the Evergreen State. Loggers, harvest hands, and clerks from Washington were sent to the trenches in Europe to fight alongside bricklayers and plumbers from Brooklyn and Boston. With the stroke of a pen, federal bureaucrats in Washington, D. C., significantly changed the life of every citizen in the other Washington. Popular crusades urged Washingtonians to buy savings bonds and to conserve fuel, wheat, and meat.

Many wartime jobs were in shipbuilding, which became a major industry on Puget Sound. The growing demand for food and timber raised the prices of those two basic resources and greatly benefited the Washington economy. But when the cost of food, housing, and other necessities rose more rapidly than wages, the economic squeeze contributed to a feeling of social and

In 1926 Bertha Landes of Seattle was elected the first woman mayor of a major city in the United States. Courtesy of Special Collections Division, University of Washington Libraries.

A flock of sheep passes over the top of Grand Coulee Dam. Courtesy of Washington State Historical Society.

political malaise.

Americans were told that the First World War was the "War to End all Wars" and "The War to Make the World Safe for Democracy." It did neither, despite the sacrifices of millions of people. An entire generation of young men was lost, and the world scarcely seemed better.

During the war, reform was equated with disloyalty, and no group felt the anger of a nation at arms more than the Wobblies. First, Americans feared German imperialism, then worldwide Communist or Bolshevik revolution, and at various times the public equated the Wobblies with both enemies.

Contributing to the worries of citizens was postwar economic unrest. In

Washington's major cities, small groups of jobless men and angry veterans organized special councils to voice their grievances. The whole process seemed suspiciously like something from the Russian Revolution of 1917.

For Washington, the year 1919 was a year of troubles. In February thousands of workers in Seattle walked off their jobs. Although it was short and nonviolent, the unprecedented Seattle General Strike frightened Americans into thinking that revolution had erupted on Puget Sound. In November a first anniversary celebration of Armistice Day turned into a violent confrontation between American Legionnaires and Wobblies in Centralia.

For all the loose talk of political revolution in Seattle in 1919, a revolution of sorts did take place at that time. It occurred on Washington's streets and highways, where the automobile forever changed the way people lived. As the public took to closed cars and new highways that made all-weather automobile travel possible, railroads, particularly the electric interurban lines radiating out of Seattle and Spokane, suffered a dramatic loss of passengers.

Overhead, a few brave passengers rode in open-cockpit planes from the cities of Washington to California on regular schedules by the late 1920s. The name Boeing became synonymous with major advances in aviation. William Boeing started his "aeroplane" shop on the shores of Lake Union in 1916, and from that modest beginning evolved the flying fortresses, stratoliners, and 747s of subsequent decades.

Although the decade of the 1920s was for many Washingtonians a time of prosperity, it opened on a sour note of economic adversity and closed the same way. The 1930s had hardly gotten underway before the Great Depression

On April 6, 1926, twenty-five hundred spectators helped Pasco celebrate the first regularly scheduled airmail service in the Pacific Northwest. The flights of Varney Air Lines linked Pasco to Boise, Idaho, and Elko, Nevada. Courtesy of Washington State University Library.

became a fact of life in Washington. Unemployment, breadlines, and poverty in a state so rich in natural resources were not easy to understand or endure.

In the search for solutions, some people embraced radical proposals and endorsed politicians who promised to enact such measures into law. One popular vehicle was the Washington Commonwealth Federation, a pressure group that operated within the Democratic Party. Although the WCF's accomplishments were really quite modest, the organization, which had as its main plank "production for use and not for profit," attracted much attention that

Troops parade on horseback at Fort Lawton, a 640-acre military facility overlooking Puget Sound on Magnolia Bluff, now Seattle's Discovery Park. Courtesy of Museum of History and Industry.

furthered the state's reputation as a hotbed of radicalism.

Organized labor was often the center of attention in 1930s Washington. Strikes were frequent and several of the largest of them tied up the waterfront. The house of labor itself erupted in a no-holds-barred power struggle between the American Federation of Labor and its aggressive young rival, the Congress of Industrial Organizations, which seceded from the AFL in mid decade. Chief strategist for the AFL forces was Seattleite Dave Beck, who emerged as one of the most powerful figures in the region and ultimately served as national head of the Teamsters Union (1952–58).

After the election of Franklin D. Roosevelt as president in 1932, the federal government became the most powerful presence in Washington State. Only once before, during the First World War, had Uncle Sam touched the lives of individual citizens in so many different ways. A host of New Deal projects provided jobs in addition to benefits ranging from cheap electrical power and water for irrigation to recreational facilities and new hospitals.

With the surprise Japanese attack on Pearl Harbor in December 1941, Washington plunged into the Second World War. Residents were confronted with change. Military service and wartime employment opportunities brought thousands of newcomers to Washington. Main streets were crowded, as were theaters, restaurants, buses, schools, and nurseries. During the first two years of the war, the shipbuilding center of Vancouver grew from twenty-five thousand to eighty-five thousand inhabitants.

During the decades following the Second World War the economic health of Washington remained linked to extractive industries, although manufacturing, trans-Pacific trade, and high-tech enterprises grew in importance. Boeing remained the Pacific Northwest's

Workers inspect the first aluminum toppings at the Reynolds plant in Longview. Courtesy of Bonneville Power Administration.

The unsightly practice of clear-cut logging is not new to Washington, as this Clark Kinsey photograph illustrates. The proper stewardship of the state's natural resources became an increasingly important topic of public debate as the century progressed. Courtesy of Special Collections Division, University of Washington Libraries.

largest manufacturer and private employer, reaching a postwar peak of 101,500 people on its Washington payroll in 1968. Computer software writing and manufacturing increased in the 1980s, with Microsoft of Bellevue and Redmond becoming a multimillion dollar enterprise and a national leader in its field.

The baby boom was perhaps the most significant of several population changes to follow the Second World War. Census statistics reveal that Washingtonians continued to move from rural to urban areas and from cities to suburban areas. Statistics show too that while the human face of Washington remained overwhelmingly Caucasian and western European in origin, important demographic changes were taking place.

In the mid 1980s, Washington had the largest non-Caucasian population of the three Pacific Northwest states, more than

10 percent of the state's total, with the fastest growing segment being Asians. This number includes a new population of refugees from Southeast Asia.

Hispanics form the region's largest minority. When the Second World War created a shortage of agricultural labor, the federal government imported male workers directly from Mexico to the Pacific Northwest. In the late 1940s more Hispanic labor arrived from the Southwest, including families lured to the Pacific Northwest by jobs. These families from Mexico permanently changed the region's minority composition.

People of Hispanic origin number at least 10 percent of the population in Yakima, Grant, Adams, and Franklin counties. Although people of Mexican origin have often been stereotyped as agricultural workers, an ever increasing number of them have found employment in white collar jobs.

People have often been attracted to

Chicano and Latino artists are a vital part of the vibrant arts scene in Washington. Alfredo Arreguin, who arrived in Washington in 1957, has had his work appear in numerous gallery and museum exhibitions. Photograph by Eduardo Calderon copyright © 1984 courtesy of the photographer.

This orderly group of Civilian Conservation Corps workers, photographed in 1933 at the Glacier CCC camp, was being trained to fight forest fires in Mount Baker National Forest.
Courtesy of National Agricultural Library.

Stylish brochures were used to promote the new planned community of Longview.
Courtesy of Washington State Historical Society.

Washington by the availability and variety of outdoor recreation and the belief that the quality of life here remains higher than in most other states. Yet environmental problems are not something that happen only back East. Each of the state's major cities has suffered from urban sprawl and air quality problems. And with each new subdivision, pressure on the environment increases, and in time population growth may destroy the desirable qualities that attracted people to Washington in the first place.

In the face of mounting population pressures and the nationalizing influence of space-age transportation and communication, an intriguing question needs to be answered: What distinguishing attributes will Washington retain in the coming decades? An unusual pattern of rainfall? Mount Saint Helens? An economy increasingly tied to Asia? A sense of Washington's heritage will help the state's residents keep their answers in perspective.

A Military Heritage

The military has maintained a substantial presence in Washington since early territorial days, when the army posted small units at strategic points to maintain order between Indians and settlers on the frontier. As late as 1908 a combined total of more than twenty-six hundred soldiers still occupied four of those forts: the Vancouver Barracks, Fort Walla Walla, Fort George Wright near Spokane, and Fort Lawton.

Four more military facilities guarded the coast: Forts Flagler, Worden, and Casey, near Port Townsend at the entrance to Admiralty Inlet, and Fort Ward, established to defend the entrance to Port Orchard, Bremerton, and the Puget Sound Naval Shipyard. Those forts, along with recruiting stations in Seattle,

Tacoma, and Spokane, and the construction of Fort Canby on the Washington side of the Columbia River, brought total War Department expenditures for 1908 to a figure that exceeded the entire state budget.

The First World War greatly expanded the shipbuilding industry and gave the state a major new military center in Pierce County: Camp (later Fort) Lewis. The county went into debt in order to present the federal government with sixty-two thousand acres for that base. Also during the war, a naval training camp was established on the University of Washington campus.

The military presence continued to grow during the twentieth century as Washington served as a point of embarkation for American personnel

In 1900 this segregated detachment was sent from Fort Lawton to the Boxer Rebellion in China. Courtesy of Special Collections Division, University of Washington Libraries.

headed into wars in Asia. The Defense Department now controls 650,000 acres of the state. The largest military installations are Fort Lewis, McChord Air Force Base, Whidbey Island Naval Air Station, Puget Sound Naval Shipyard at Bremerton, Fairchild Air Force Base, and the Naval Submarine Base at Bangor.

Fort Worden, one of a trio of military facilities intended to guard the coast near Port Townsend, is now a state park, where weeds grow through cracks in the now silent gun emplacements. Photograph by Torka's Studio, Port Townsend, courtesy of Special Collections Division, University of Washington Libraries.

Soldiers at Camp Lewis learn the trench warfare of the First World War in this view from a souvenir picture folder. Courtesy of Special Collections Division, University of Washington Libraries.

The First World War at Home

First World War enlisted men line up for duty at Seattle's Union Station.
Courtesy of Museum of History and Industry.

Here on Puget Sound, a great Western city is devoting its energies to the construction of ships and is achieving a success commensurate with its desire to aid the nation in this crisis." The crisis to which this *Seattle Times* editorial referred in September 1918 was the First World War. On the home front, Washingtonians built ships, bought Liberty bonds ($31 million in King County alone), and participated in numerous other projects "to aid the nation."

By 1918 seven shipyards on Puget Sound employed thirty-two thousand workers and produced 20 percent of the nation's wartime tonnage. Workers thronged to Puget Sound from other western states. When Butte mayor W. H. "Billie" Maloney visited the Seattle yards where some three thousand former Montana residents were employed, he quipped that "half of Butte seems to have moved to Seattle."

In addition to shipyard workers and the

CO-OPERATIVE EXTENSION WORK IN AGRICULTURE AND HOME ECONOMICS, STATE COLLEGE OF WASHINGTON AND UNITED STATES DEPARTMENT OF AGRICULTURE CO-OPERATING

YOU CAN HELP PREVENT

FOOD SHORTAGE IN U. S.

Plant every acre of summer-fallow that will produce a crop to corn, beans, peas or potatoes.

Solve the meat problem by keeping the brood sows, lambs, veal calves and laying hens.

Every home should have a year's supply of home canned meats, vegetables and fruits.

Every boy and girl should have a flock of chickens, a pen of rabbits or a garden.

EVERY FAMILY SHOULD HAVE A GOOD GARDEN
EVERY FARM A BIG PATCH OF POTATOES AND BEANS

STATE COLLEGE OF WASHINGTON
EXTENSION SERVICE

Will send you FREE information on
Gardening, Livestock, Farming, Poultry, Home Economics, Canning
WRITE: W. S. THORNBER, DIRECTOR, PULLMAN, WASH.
OR YOUR COUNTY AGRICULTURAL AGENT IF YOU HAVE ONE

Washington citizens were urged to conserve food and plant larger crops to support the war effort, but the collapse of grain prices in late 1920 proved costly to many a patriotic farmer who had borrowed money to acquire land and equipment when prices were higher. Courtesy of National Agricultural Library.

nearly 30,000 men who joined in the Spruce Production Division, 66,870 Washingtonians enlisted in military service. Women helped alleviate the resulting labor shortages in agriculture and industry. The war reached into every resident's life, bringing food shortages and stimulating Liberty bond and Red Cross drives.

On college campuses, student training corps rushed their cadets through navy and army programs. At the University of Washington the Student Army Training Corps offered courses in mapmaking and topography, military mathematics, and military French to students who were enlisted as privates.

Individuals who spoke out against the war faced censure from their neighbors. Anna Louise Strong, an opponent of the war, lost a recall election and her seat on the Seattle school board in March 1918. Schools throughout the state banned the teaching of German. Immigrant churches offered services in English rather than German.

During those years another national crisis, the Spanish influenza epidemic, touched the life of every Washingtonian. The experience of mobilizing the state for war proved useful in combatting the 1918–19 epidemic. Public health officials also drew upon the experiences of Eastern cities such as Philadelphia and Boston, which had suffered the epidemic several months before it reached the Pacific Northwest. The Seattle Health Department promoted masks as a way to stop the disease from spreading.

To contain the plague, cities and towns

"I have bought a Liberty bond—have you?" From Bundles to Britain to bond drives and war work, buttons got the message across during the First World War.
Courtesy of Eastern Washington State Historical Society.

throughout the state closed public places of all kinds, from pool halls to churches and schools. Because of bans on public gatherings, Thanksgiving festivities had to be canceled in some parts of the Northwest. In the end, five hundred thousand to seven hundred thousand Americans died of influenza, in contrast to the nation's First World War death toll of fifty thousand.

Women rivet heaters and passers at the Puget Sound Naval Shipyard, 1919. Courtesy of National Archives.

Masked under orders from the health department, a Seattle newsboy stands in front of one of the city's theaters closed to help prevent the spread of the influenza epidemic. Courtesy of Museum of History and Industry.

The Spruce Production Division:
Uncle Sam in the Woods

Troops from the Spruce Production Division near Lake Crescent on the Olympic Peninsula. Courtesy of Washington State Historical Society.

Wobblies were conducting their most successful strike in the woods of Washington when America entered the First World War. Theirs was a novel protest that consisted mainly of remaining on the job but working at the slowest possible pace. The slowdown drove the timber industry to its wit's end before the war gave management a powerful new ally in Uncle Sam.

Spruce was a light, strong wood needed for aircraft production. British and French manufacturers purchased huge quantities. The federal government thus considered spruce vital to the war effort and was in no mood to tolerate a strike.

The government responded to the Wobbly slowdown with a two-fisted attack. It created a military organization, the Spruce Production Division headed by Colonel Brice P. Disque, which put twenty-seven thousand soldiers to work in the lumber camps, and a civilian Loyal Legion of Loggers and Lumbermen (4-L) that was essentially an enormous company union. During the summer of 1917 the Loyal Legion attracted some one hundred thousand members who signed a patriotic pledge not to strike. Together those two organizations cut the needed spruce and other lumber.

Wobbly membership declined precipitously not only as a result of the Spruce Production Division and the 4-L but also from federal raids and vigilante attacks on its meeting halls and leaders. Ironically, the presence of U. S. troops in the lumber camps resulted in many improvements that Wobblies had long sought, including the eight-hour day, shower facilities, and clean bunkhouses.

1919: Year of Discontent

The First World War armistice on November 11, 1918, left Seattle workers frustrated. During the war, a uniform scale had kept the wages of Seattle's many shipyard workers stable. But inflation eroded the value of wages that had already been stretched thin by Seattle's high living costs. Moreover, wartime wage controls remained in place. Early the following year their discontent resulted in an unprecedented general strike.

On Thursday morning, February 6, 1919, sixty-five thousand strikers quit work; another forty thousand workers remained at home. Commercial traffic, including streetcars, halted for four days. Restaurants and some schools were closed, but hospitals remained open, the electricity stayed on, and newspapers published abbreviated editions.

Leaders urged workers to be peaceful, and there was no disorder. "We are undertaking the most tremendous move ever made by *Labor* in this country," activist Anna Louise Strong wrote in the *Union Record,* "a move which will lead *no one knows where!*" Strikers maintained twelve kitchens to sell food at low cost and opened milk stations to provide for babies and invalids.

Mayor Ole Hanson branded the strike a revolution and threatened martial law,

Mayor Ole Hanson called the Seattle general strike a "revolution," and the city mobilized its police force in anticipation of the coming strike. Courtesy of Museum of History and Industry.

Strikers maintained milk stations for babies and small children, twelve kitchens that served cooked food, and stations for grocery supplies, such as the one shown here, photographed on Friday, February 7, 1919. Courtesy of Museum of History and Industry.

while various groups formed to express concern or plan vigilante action. But on Monday the workers returned to their jobs. Later that year the state legislature enacted laws to punish sabotage and criminal syndicalism, as well as the display of flags or insignia of groups hostile to the government.

On November 11, 1919, the first anniversary of the First World War armistice, violence erupted in Centralia, a timber town of seventy-five hundred. Responding to rumors that the IWW headquarters would be raided during the American Legion's Armistice Day parade, the Wobblies armed themselves to defend their hall.

When the parade halted briefly in front of the building, shots were fired on both sides, and four Legionnaires fell to the ground, fatally wounded. That night vigilantes terrorized Wobbly prisoners held in the Centralia jail and seized Wesley Everest, a U. S. Army veteran, and hanged him from a nearby railroad bridge. After a celebrated trial in Montesano, the court convicted eight Wobblies of second degree murder and sentenced them to lengthy prison terms. The last of the jailed Wobblies was not released until 1939.

Although the Seattle Star, *one of the city's most popular newspapers, had a generally progressive and pro-labor reputation, it opposed the general strike.* Courtesy of Special Collections Division, University of Washington Libraries.

The Auto Age

When automobiles first appeared on Washington roads, they seemed only a fad. More often than not, they were owned by the wealthy elite.

Originally sold by bicycle dealers, the early "gas-burners" attracted crowds of admirers and skeptics wherever they appeared. Pioneer motorists had to deal with muddy roads, inadequate direction signs, and balky engines.

A total of 9,300 Washingtonians owned a car by 1910, but that still amounted to only one vehicle for every 157 residents. Ten years later, however, one of every eight Washingtonians owned a car. By the early 1920s, the automobile had become a routine part of life.

In rural Washington, the motor vehicle meant less isolation and greater mobility for residents, as well as a decline in small

An early service station at Stevens Pass at the crest of the Cascades in the mid 1920s.
Courtesy of Minnesota Historical Society.

market towns. In urban areas, the development of suburbs and shopping centers after the Second World War signified the public's increasing dependence on private transportation.

The story of the automobile is closely linked to that of highways. In early Washington, transportation between towns was limited to waterways and crude trails. One of the first agencies the new state established was the Highway Department. During the first sixteen years of statehood, the department spent $132,000 to develop county roads. But to many people that was inadequate. After the turn of the century, the University of

The steam ferry SS Leschi *on Lake Washington in 1931.* Courtesy of Museum of History and Industry.

The hazards of city driving are captured by a photographer from Spokane's Libby Studio; here a crowd gathers at Fourteenth and Grand to witness the results of a dramatic 1929 streetcar-automobile crash. Courtesy of Eastern Washington State Historical Society.

Although the Bothell road had been surfaced with "Warrenite" in the fall of 1911, it was worn out and in need of replacement by this crew of men, photographed working on May 8, 1912. This road cost $17,000 per mile! Courtesy of Special Collections Division, University of Washington Libraries.

Washington instituted a chair in roadbuilding to bring modern expertise to the state and overcome a major impediment to economic development.

The federal government aided highway construction with topographic surveys, begun in Washington in 1893. By 1909 twenty-seven quadrangles comprising 18,400 square miles had been surveyed. Still, only a few roads were constructed before 1916, and many of those dead-ended in the mountains. That year, after designing a plan for interconnecting roads, Washington received federal money to build the foundation of its present state highway system.

Tourism and the Great Outdoors

When Pacific Coast fairs and expositions, such as Seattle's Alaska-Yukon-Pacific Exposition of 1909, drew visitors to the state, interest groups of all kinds attempted to detour them to their own communities. "Stop off in Spokane," suggested one typical pamphlet. The economic benefits of tourism included not only the money spent by visitors but also potential investments in real estate and development.

People with time and money for travel have long enjoyed Washington's spectacular scenery and the outdoor recreation that water and mountains offer. Early tourists used stagecoaches and railroads to visit the sights. The Great Northern and Northern Pacific railroads often offered special tourist packages. At James Longmire's hot springs spa on Mount Rainier or the elegant hotel at "Sol Duc" Hot Springs in the Olympic Range, guests from all over the world enjoyed relaxing baths and good fishing.

State residents also contributed to the tourist trade. Urban dwellers on Puget Sound escaped city life by vacationing on

City and county pleasures were promoted as vacation ideas by Washington publications such as this Tourist's Guide to Spokane and Environs. Courtesy of Washington State Historical Society.

Tourists headed for the large and elegant Sol Duc Hot Springs Hotel in the Olympics over land and by boat. Courtesy of Library of Congress.

In the mid 1920s the lodge at Mount Baker offered magnificent scenery, a large granite fireplace, and water sports for those inclined to rush the season and swim in a partially frozen lake.
Photograph by Burt Huntoon courtesy of Special Collections Division, University of Washington Libraries.

nearby islands or in the mountains. Beaches and lakes, such as Liberty Lake outside Spokane, were popular spots for boating, swimming, fishing, and picnicking, especially when made accessible by public transportation. With the increase in automobile ownership in the early twentieth century, touring and camping became fashionable middle-class summer activities.

Washingtonians, such as this family out for the Fourth of July in 1923, took their cars to the beaches and devised rigs to make them serve for camping and picnicking. Courtesy of Special Collections Division, University of Washington Libraries.

Parks and Recreation

Washington's national parks mirror the fascination of state residents with their physical environment. Today the three national parks and two national recreation areas of Washington offer spectacular and unique vistas, flora, and fauna. The state's national historic sites open windows on the past.

Mount Rainier National Park, founded in 1898, epitomized the national parks of the late nineteenth century. It was a "mountain-top" park preserved for the spectacular scenery it contained. It also suited the needs of the Northern Pacific Railway, which traded marginally productive land in the park for its choice of federal land in other parts of the state served by its tracks. In the 1890s national

Tourists at the Nisqually entrance to Mount Rainier in 1912. Photograph by Asahel Curtis courtesy of Washington State Historical Society.

parks were the result of happenstance as much as planning, and the creation of Rainier was a tribute both to its beauty and the persistence of Washingtonians and the Northern Pacific.

Theodore Roosevelt established the Mount Olympus National Monument in 1909 during his last days in office. It was created to protect more than scenery; the area was home to the Olympic elk, also known as the Roosevelt elk, which had been decimated by extensive hunting at the end of the nineteenth century.

The legislation creating the monument contained few restrictions on commercial

Long before nylon, aluminum, and plastic equipment, Washingtonians responded to the challenge of the mountains and glaciers. Asahel Curtis photographed these hikers about 1919. Courtesy of Special Collections Division, University of Washington Libraries.

A ranger on horseback patrols the Olympic National Park. Courtesy of Special Collections Division, University of Washington Libraries.

use of its resources, and development on the Olympic Peninsula continued largely unabated. Powerful timber and mining interests opposed the monument, and President Woodrow Wilson halved its size in 1915. Twenty-three years later the newly established Olympic National Park encompassed a large portion of the deleted area.

During the 1930s the focus of American preservation changed from natural to historic. The federal Historic Sites Act of 1935 led to the establishment of the Whitman Mission National Monument, later renamed a national historic site.

The North Cascades National Park and the adjacent Lake Chelan and Ross Lake national recreation areas are the latest additions to Washington's national park

areas, although agitation for a national park in the Lake Chelan area had begun as early as 1902. Following the Second World War, unspoiled areas such as the North Cascades became more and more rare, and Washingtonians sought to preserve them. The park was designed to be as free of physical development as possible. Despite their unsullied beauty, the North Cascades were reserved more for their purity than uniqueness.

Asahel Curtis photographed this fishing scene on the Green River in about 1915, as publicity for the Northern Pacific Railway. Courtesy of Library of Congress.

City, state, and county parks as well as national parks afford Washingtonians the opportunity to enjoy the spectacular beauty the state has to offer. Riverfront Park in the heart of downtown Spokane, the site of EXPO '74, teems with joggers, bikers, and business people on their lunch hours.

The development of Seattle's outstanding park system began with donations of scattered tracts of land. In 1884, David Denny and his wife gave the city the five acres that eventually became Denny Park. Six years later, the new board

This scenic portrait of Mount Rainier from Lake Washington Boulevard combines the spectacular natural setting of Seattle with the talents of John C. Olmsted, the landscape architect, and Asahel Curtis, the photographer. Courtesy of Washington State Historical Society.

For over a century, Seattle's parks have bustled with boaters and promenaders on pleasant days. This is Leschi Park before 1907. Courtesy of Museum of History and Industry.

of park commissioners established its headquarters there and soon acquired the land on north Capitol Hill that was first called City Park and later, Volunteer Park. Like Guy Phinney's Woodland Park, which was privately owned until 1900 but free to all who obeyed the posted rules, Volunteer Park was outside the city limits but accessible by streetcar.

In 1903, the park board hired the fashionable East Coast firm of the Olmsted Brothers to design a boulevard system. The Olmsteds were the sons of Frederick Law Olmsted, the influential landscape architect who planned New York's Central Park and the Chicago World's Fair of 1893, and who in 1873 had proposed an overall plan for Tacoma that was never adopted. Like their father, the sons favored curving roads that followed natural contours, leaving some areas wild while creating formal designs in others with shrubbery, flower beds, and artificial bodies of water.

John C. Olmsted recommended a long-range plan that involved buying new

property and winding a parkway around Seattle to link the existing municipal parks and new parks to be bought from private interests. His reports won voter approval for the $4 million in bonds that were sold between 1905 and 1912 to finance the acquisition and landscaping of parkland and the building of most of the tree-lined road he had proposed.

By 1909 Seattle had fourteen parks, some with lawns and formal gardens, others with wooded ravines and hillsides. The parks provided picnic areas and places for swimming and boating, but many spots could be reached only by automobile or water, restricting their use to people who could afford cars or boats.

The parks that could be reached by streetcar teemed with merrymakers who rented boats, crowded city beaches, and walked the boardwalks in west Seattle and along Lake Washington. One early twentieth century writer described Madison Park as "a Coney Island . . . a playground for the Industrials, a breathing spot for the Employed."

Great Depression and New Deal

The 1930s were years of despair. The Great Depression, the national economic crisis heralded by the stock market crash of 1929, created personal hardship and community distress throughout Washington. Without markets for their products, lumber mills, grain growers, canneries and other Washington producers faced failure and foreclosure. With almost 25 percent of the work force unemployed, relief lines, soup kitchens, and "Hoovervilles"—shantytowns at the outskirts of many cities—became familiar sights.

City, county, and state resources proved inadequate to deal with the crisis. The election of 1932 placed Franklin Delano Roosevelt in the White House and brought a New Deal to Washington.

Evidence of federal "alphabet soup" programs—from the AAA (Agricultural

"Hoovervilles," such as this one in Seattle, were dramatic, visible signs of Depression problems such as homelessness, unemployment, foreclosures, and economic failures. Courtesy of Special Collections Division, University of Washington Libraries.

Adjustment Administration) to the WPA (Works Progress Administration)— became visible throughout the state. Blue Eagle symbols appeared in store windows to identify businesses whose owners followed National Recovery Administration guidelines for minimum wages and maximum hours. WPA projects

In February 1931 Seattle's unemployed rallied outside the County-City Building to protest "Hoover's Hunger Regime." Courtesy of Special Collections Division, University of Washington Libraries.

Bread lines appeared in Seattle, Spokane, and other localities during the Great Depression. Estimates of unemployment in Seattle ranged from 23 to 60 percent. Painting by Ronald Debs Ginther courtesy of Washington State Historical Society.

employed artists, historians, actors, writers, musicians, and others to create a variety of public works that ranged from murals to theater productions.

People went to work to construct new bridges, irrigation systems, and other large-scale projects, including the Grand Coulee Dam, under the guidance of the Public Works Administration. Meanwhile the Civilian Conservation Corps employed an army of eighteen- to twenty-five-year-old men to develop forests, parks, and recreation areas. Housed in camps, the CCC cadets blazed trails, laid telephone lines, planted trees, built fire lookout towers, and constructed roads. The pay was thirty dollars each month, of which twenty-five dollars was sent home to their families.

Not all New Deal programs were successful. The AAA plan to control nationwide wheat production by paying benefits to farmers who agreed to reduce their wheat acreage by 20 percent was

least successful in Washington. Even after its implementation, the harvests of 1934 and 1935 produced a serious surplus of grain in the Pacific Northwest.

This busy pay office, its walls adorned with Franklin D. Roosevelt's photograph, a WPA poster, and a 1939 calendar, symbolizes the hopeful promise of the New Deal. Courtesy of Special Collections Division, University of Washington Libraries.

Electricity: From White Coal to Nuclear Power

In 1885, just three years after Thomas Edison first demonstrated the commercial possibilities of his electric invention, Spokane Falls had electric lights. One of the first cities west of the Mississippi to illuminate its streets with electricity, the city utilized water power from the nearby falls to operate its dynamo. The visual impact of the illumination was dramatic; as newcomer William Emsely Jackson recalled, "I can never forget my feelings that first night as we looked out over the city and saw the bright arc lights in all directions. . . . We then realized that we were to make our home in a real city."

Other Washington cities rapidly acquired this latest symbol of modern civilization. Both Seattle and Tacoma established incandescent lighting systems in 1886. Streetcars and interurban railroads, elevators, and factories soon made use of electrical power.

The environmental impact of electric power was also dramatic. Hydroelectric dams, transmission lines, and multistoried

Stringing wires high above the streets, this turn-of-the-century Seattle Electric Company crew helped provide energy for the city's rapidly increasing population, which at that time numbered more than eighty thousand. Courtesy of Museum of History and Industry.

factories literally transformed the state's landscape. Urban dwellers initially reaped most of the benefits of electricity, but with the establishment of the Rural Electrification Administration of 1935 many Washington villages and farms also acquired electricity.

The promise of water power that had lured early settlers to the Columbia River region also intrigued President Franklin D. Roosevelt. Federal and state involvement in power generation grew during the Roosevelt years, sometimes competing with private Eastern companies that had initially dominated the production of hydroelectricity.

During the 1930s Washington received far more than the national average of New Deal public works money for reclamation, navigation, and hydroelectric projects on

Long Lake Dam—located on the Spokane River—had the highest spillways and most powerful turbines in the world at the time of its construction. It is still producing electricity for the Washington Water Power Company. Courtesy of Washington State Historical Society.

the Columbia River. These improvements offered hope and employment to millions of jobless Americans who were victims of the Great Depression and the Dust Bowl.

The first of the great new dams were Bonneville and Grand Coulee, built by the Army Corps of Engineers and the Bureau of Reclamation, respectively. Each dam, reflecting the mission of the lead agency, had a particular objective in addition to providing jobs and power. The locks of Bonneville—named for a fur trader and army explorer of the 1830s—facilitated river commerce, and Grand Coulee provided water for irrigation. Since neither agency was in the business of marketing electricity, the Bonneville Power Administration was created in 1937 to distribute the power generated by the just completed Bonneville Dam.

The BPA was intended to be a temporary distribution agency until such time as Congress approved a Columbia Valley Authority, a Northwest equivalent of the famous redevelopment agency of the Southeast, the Tennessee Valley Authority. But a CVA would never happen. Political squabbling between private and public power interests, infighting between federal agencies, and a general fear of government centralization doomed this proposal.

Nevertheless, Columbia River hydroelectric power inaugurated a new industrial era for the Northwest. Low-cost electricity attracted both private and public facilities. Many of these operations, as well as Grand Coulee Dam itself, started production at about the time America entered into the Second World War.

When the United States became the arsenal of democracy, the Bonneville and Grand Coulee dams helped to power it. The aluminum fashioned into Boeing aircraft and the Liberty ships welded together in the shipyards of the Columbia River and Puget Sound provided America both its wartime wings and a vital lifeline.

Columbia River power from Grand

Spokane promoters capitalized on the city's abundance of hydroelectric power. Courtesy of Washington State Historical Society.

HYDRO = ELECTRIC DEVELOPMENT
PUGET SOUND POWER & LIGHT COMPANY

BELLINGHAM   SEATTLE
EVERETT   TACOMA
EXECUTIVE OFFICES   SEATTLE, WASH.

The waters of Snoqualmie Falls started generating electricity in 1898. As of 1987, the original generators were still producing their rated output of six thousand watts for the Puget Sound Power and Light Company.
Courtesy of Special Collections Division, University of Washington Libraries.

Coulee Dam dictated the selection of southeastern Washington as the home of the Hanford Project, which was investigating military applications of atomic energy. In 1941 a few hundred farmers and villagers lived in the Richland area, while at the height of wartime research and construction fifty-one thousand people called it home.

As tangible a contribution as the Bonneville and Grand Coulee dams were able to make to the industrialization of Washington during the 1940s, it was a natural disaster that furthered the completion of the system of dams on the Columbia River. The spring runoff in May 1948 raised the river to the highest level recorded since 1894. On Memorial Day the dikes along the river in the vicinity of

Portland broke, destroying millions of dollars in property and leaving dozens of people dead.

Grand Coulee and Bonneville were unable to stem the torrent of water that streamed down from the tributaries. The Vanport Flood, as it is called (after the war workers' boom town on the Oregon side of the river, named for the juxtaposition of Vancouver and Portland), combined with recurrent brownouts, created a political environment that made possible a dozen or more dams on the Columbia River system.

After two decades of dam building in the 1950s and 1960s, public power generally, and the BPA specifically, became overconfident of its ability to project power needs and manage technology. When the Columbia's hydroelectric potential appeared "exhausted," the Northwest's power planners turned to nuclear energy as a new energy source.

The Washington Public Power Supply System, formed by sixteen public utility districts in 1957, was originally a low budget operation. It successfully built a hydroelectric plant at Packwood Lake in the Cascades and a nuclear plant on the Hanford Reservation. From there it plunged into the construction of five nuclear plants and in the process became the largest issuer of tax-free municipal bonds in American history.

During the 1980s many things went wrong with the WPPSS program. As of mid decade, two of the nuclear units had been abandoned, two had been mothballed, and only one plant produced electricity. The financial woes of the Washington Public Power Supply System are in many ways a sad tale of the technological euphoria of earlier decades gone astray.

Grand Coulee Dam

*S*he winds down her granite canyon
and she bends across the lea
    Like a silver, running stallion
down her seaway to the sea;
    Cast your eye upon the greatest
thing yet built by human hands,
    On the King Columbia river, it's that big
Grand Coulee dam.

These are the words of folk singer
Woody Guthrie. Hired for a month in
1941 by the Bonneville Power
Administration, Guthrie visited the dam
while it was still under construction. He
chronicled the massive undertaking in a
series of songs including "Roll On,
Columbia," "Jackhammer John," and "My
Uniform's My Dirty Overhalls."

The Grand Coulee Dam began in 1933
with $63 million allotted from the Public
Works Administration. It formed the
centerpiece of an ambitious irrigation plan
known as the Columbia Basin Project,
designed to create a farmer's paradise in
central Washington.

Pneumatic drilling hoses snake around this 1938 Grand Coulee Dam crew during one of the early stages of construction. Courtesy of Eastern Washington State Historical Society.

This floating camp housed workers logging the area that was soon to be inundated by the waters of "Lake Roosevelt," backing up behind Grand Coulee Dam. Courtesy of Special Collections Division, University of Washington Libraries.

Facing page: This 1942 image of a workman dwarfed by the massive waterfall pouring over the Grand Coulee Dam dramatizes the power and size of "the greatest thing yet built by human hands." Courtesy of Library of Congress.

THE GRAND COULEE DAM. Words and music by Woody Guthrie. TRO © copyright 1958 (renewed 1963) and 1963 Ludlow Music, Inc. New York, NY. Used by permission.

Named "the greatest thing yet built by human hands" or "the eighth wonder of the modern world," the Grand Coulee Dam was indeed grand. "Man and machinery produce a harmony of motion, building night and day without pause," boasted one souvenir pamphlet.

Two observation areas overlooked the worksite. Visitors watched more than seven thousand laborers, managers, and engineers at work setting world construction records as they excavated 45 million cubic yards of earth, used 130 million board feet of lumber, and poured 10 million cubic yards of concrete.

Not only was the Grand Coulee the largest concrete dam in the world, but the project provided eastern Washington with a needed economic boost. The first excavation jobs went to men of Grant, Douglas, Lincoln, and other nearby counties hit hard by the Great Depression. To house workers and a support staff, a number of new towns—including Mason City and Grand Coulee—sprang up near the dam.

But not everyone benefited from the project. The dam's construction and rising waters in Lake Roosevelt, which was backing up behind Grand Coulee,

Grand Coulee Dam not only provided jobs during the depressed years of the 1930s, but also curbed Columbia River floods, generated electric power and provided water for a new 1,200,000-acre Garden of Eden. Courtesy of Special Collections Division, University of Washington Libraries.

This 1950 Bureau of Reclamation aerial photograph shows not only the dam and the upper Grand Coulee, but also the pumping plant and siphons that channeled water to the Columbia Basin Project. Courtesy of National Archives.

displaced ten towns—Daisy, Marcus, Kettle Falls, Inchelium, and others—and more than three thousand people, including Native Americans living on the Colville Reservation.

The water impounded by the dam covered Kettle Falls, where generations of Colville Indians and other Salish peoples had fished for salmon under treaty provisions. The day the waters of Lake Roosevelt covered the falls, the Colville Indians held a "ceremony of tears." Because the high dam was built without fish ladders, its completion ended the salmon spawning runs along the upper Columbia River.

At 2:30 p.m. on June 1, 1942, fifteen thousand people gathered to watch the first water pour over the spillway. Conceived originally as a way to provide jobs for the unemployed and water for irrigated farming, the Grand Coulee Dam became even more important as a source of power for wartime production. By the end of the Second World War, it had become the planet's largest single source of electricity.

Photographer Wallace Gamble captured the Colville Indians' ceremonial final stick game at Kettle Falls before rising dam waters engulfed their lands. Courtesy of Eastern Washington State Historical Society.

The Columbia Basin Project

The Grand Coulee Dam formed an integral part of a far-reaching plan to irrigate and thereby transform arid sections of central and eastern Washington into productive farm lands. Stretching across more than a million acres from Pasco to Ephrata, the Columbia Basin Project formed a network of canals and roads linking farm communities and cities. Boosters hoped the land would in time support five hundred thousand people.

The project required existing owners to sell all but 160 acres of their lands to the Bureau of Reclamation at pre-water prices in return for cheap water. The government then resold the land in forty-, sixty-, or eighty-acre parcels to new settlers. Later the maximum size of project farms was increased to 320 acres.

Plans to lay out new towns and transportation systems, to create a new utopian community of small farmers, and to combine technological advances with agrarian ideals have not been entirely realized. In addition to political setbacks and financial difficulties, environmental realities have dimmed the project's vision. Pouring dam water over arid lands with poor drainage has led to excessive salt buildup in the soil.

Nonetheless, the Columbia Basin Project continues to reflect New Deal dreams. As of the early 1980s the project's 540,000 irrigated acres produced more than sixty different crops.

Looking south from the Grand Coulee Dam, this map depicts the relationship between the dam and the Columbia Basin Project lands. Courtesy of Special Collections Division, University of Washington Libraries.

An irrigated field of potatoes near Quincy on the Columbia Basin Project. Courtesy of Museum of History and Industry.

A laborer turns water into a field of sugar-beets. Courtesy of National Archives.

A workman inspects the interior of one of the many siphons that carried irrigation water from the Grand Coulee Dam. Courtesy of Special Collections Division, University of Washington Libraries.

The Second World War

The Vancouver Shipyard, like its two counterparts across the Columbia in Portland, was established by Henry J. Kaiser to build small aircraft carriers and supply freighters known as "Liberty ships." Courtesy of Oregon Historical Society.

T he Second World War played a major role in the modern era of Washington's history. Few states experienced more rapid and intense changes; wartime social and economic dislocation left no community untouched.

Change was most visible in Washington's two largest centers of war production—Puget Sound with its aircraft and shipbuilding industries, and Vancouver where Henry J. Kaiser's shipyards established world records for production. Most improbable of all was the war's impact on Hanford, a hamlet in central Washington that disappeared when the federal government and a force of forty-five thousand workers erected a multimillion dollar complex to produce plutonium for the world's first atomic bombs.

Industries large and small contributed to an outpouring of ships, barges, aircraft, metals, food, machinery, clothing, munitions, armaments, lumber, and various kinds of wood products. Seattle alone secured war contracts totaling $5.6 billion, ranking it among the nation's top three cities in per capita war orders.

Pacific Car and Foundry (now PACCAR) in Renton converted from making logging trucks to Sherman tanks. Eighty-eight shipyards in Washington, including the U. S. Navy's big facility at Bremerton, employed a total of 150,000 workers in 1944.

War industries wrought profound population changes and so, too, did military installations. The state contained an assortment of more than fifty relatively large army and navy bases, with military personnel concentrated mainly in the Fort

As it did in the other twentieth century wars, Seattle served as a point of embarkment for American troops serving in the Pacific during the Second World War. These are members of the U.S. Army Signal Corps going aboard ship, February 10, 1945. Courtesy of Museum of History and Industry.

Lewis/Camp Murray/McChord Field area south of Tacoma. New military bases caused population booms that nearly overwhelmed smaller communities such as Ephrata, Soap Lake, Moses Lake, and Oak Harbor.

With Washington located nearer the Pacific conflict than most other states and several vital war industries installed here, residents greatly feared invasion and air raids. Antisubmarine nets were strung across Puget Sound, and Boeing cleverly camouflaged its sprawling factories to resemble a residential area from the air. Because of wartime hysteria and long-standing anti-Asian prejudice, Japanese Americans living west of the Cascades were interned in remote camps in the interior.

The Second World War brought social dislocation, privation, and death to Washingtonians. It also created unprecedented prosperity and a rare sense of common national purpose. Not since that time have Americans been so united in the conviction that they were fighting a "good war" to defeat unmitigated evil. Such a belief, reinforced in countless ways by patriotic exhortations and demonstrations, helped Washingtonians adjust to rationing, high prices, overcrowded trains and streetcars, and news of destruction and death.

"Timberettes" working for the Snoqualmie Falls Lumber Company. During the Second World War women held a wide range of jobs in Northwest sawmills, despite the critics who charged that the work was fit only for husky men. Courtesy of Forest History Society.

Japanese American Relocation

o Japs Wanted." The hand-painted sign scrawled across the garage door of a Japanese American home in Seattle dates from May 1945. It reflects not only the strong anti-Japanese sentiment prevalent during and immediately after the Second World War, but also a deep-rooted prejudice toward Asians in the United States. In nineteenth and early twentieth century Washington, alien land laws, immigration restrictions, and exclusionary naturalization policies deprived Asian Americans of the rights their neighbors took for granted.

After Japan bombed Pearl Harbor, a combination of panic and prejudice led to the wartime internment of most Washingtonians of Japanese ancestry. For more than seven thousand Puget Sound residents, Executive Order 9066 meant an abrupt disruption of their lives. They were ordered to register and report in May

1942 to the Puyallup evacuation center, named Camp Harmony by the army. After two to four months in the hastily constructed camp at the state fairgrounds most were sent to Minidoka in semiarid southern Idaho for the duration of the war.

Few Japanese Americans resisted their removal from the "war zone" along the coast. For some, the removal was a way to escape the racial tension that had escalated after Pearl Harbor. Others accepted the governmental directive as a way to assert their support of the United States. Quaker Gordon Hirabayashi was one of the few who challenged U. S. policy. In the end, the United States Supreme Court ruled against Hirabayashi, who served fifteen months in prison for violating a Japanese-only curfew and refusing to take oaths.

As the sense of panic lessened in 1943, some internees were released from the

"No Japs Wanted," May 29, 1945. Courtesy of Museum of History and Industry.

Tagged with numbers, a mother and child await evacuation from Bainbridge Island in 1942. Courtesy of Museum of History and Industry.

camps to attend school or to work. A special all-Nisei army combat unit was sent to Europe, where it served with distinction.

The relocation centers closed down in 1945 but their legacy continued. Two-thirds of those imprisoned during the war chose to return to their former Washington homes. While some found their property intact, others faced the difficult task of reconstructing their lives after the loss of lands, jobs, and homes. Some internees, embittered by their experience, moved to Japan.

The belongings of Japanese and Japanese Americans stored in the basement of the Tacoma Buddhist Church were pilfered during the war years. Courtesy of National Archives.

Hanford and the A-Bomb

O n August 6, 1945, President Harry S Truman informed the American public that the United States had dropped an atomic bomb on Hiroshima, Japan. That announcement also revealed for the first time what a group of wartime employees in eastern Washington had been producing at a secret plant. Weapons-grade plutonium from the Hanford Engineer Works, a part of the Manhattan Project, fueled the war-ending bomb that fell on Nagasaki.

News media rushed to the desolate site along the Columbia River. There they found a city of prefabricated housing owned by the federal government.

This July 1948 Atomic Energy Commission aerial photograph shows the extensive "living quarters of the people who staff the Hanford Works, world center of plutonium production." Courtesy of National Archives.

It was home to fifteen thousand Hanford employees. Nearby, a construction camp with mess halls, recreation facilities, and barracks for as many as forty-five thousand workers appeared like a mirage in the midst of a landscape of irrigated farms. The production reactors, cooled by Columbia River water and fueled by electricity from the Grand Coulee Dam, stood behind miles of fences.

"We're Here to Stay—Where we work, where we live, and where we play," was the theme of the 1947 Richland Day celebration. The cover of their souvenir brochure reveals the "atom bustin' " village's continuing close identification with the nuclear industry during the cold war years. Courtesy of Washington State Historical Society.

A Hanford workman models "the newest safety device which is used to report the level of radiation in an extremely 'hot' zone." Like other publicity photographs released by the government during the 1950s, this image emphasized the safety of atomic energy in an attempt to sell nuclear power to a postwar United States. Courtesy of National Archives.

After the war the plant remained active under the direction of General Electric, the government contractor that replaced DuPont in 1945. The habit of secrecy also remained in effect with the continued production of weapons-grade plutonium during the cold war. In the city of Richland , "the Atomic City," residents celebrated both their economic security based on the Hanford contracts and their postwar civic independence from federal regulations, although it was as late as 1957 before they were allowed to buy their government-owned homes.

Secrecy combined with a lack of complete knowledge about the effects or dangers of radiation and other toxic substances led to questionable disposal practices during the 1940s and 1950s. Only recently has detailed information been released about the massive emissions of potentially harmful radiation into the atmosphere, soil, and water. These disclosures, along with the nuclear accident at Three Mile Island, the Chernobyl disaster, and the local controversy over the Washington Public Power Supply System, have raised disturbing questions about the nuclear reservation.

The Boeing Company

The main currents of world history are not always apparent in the fortunes of individual states, but Washington and its chief corporate citizen, the giant Boeing Commercial Airplane Company, are exceptions to that rule.

Much like the arrival of the transcontinental railroads, the two world wars had a revolutionary impact on the economy of Washington. When the federal government needed training planes to prepare for involvement in the First World War, it entered into its first contract with William Boeing's tiny enterprise in Seattle. War work stabilized the company's operations and laid the foundation for a long association between Boeing and Uncle Sam.

Boeing, like the state of Washington, matured during the Second World War.

At the peak of wartime production in 1944, Boeing employed fifty thousand men and women. An armada of B-17 "Flying Fortresses" and B-29 "Super Fortresses" rolled off the final assembly lines in Seattle and turned the tide in the air war over Europe and the South Pacific.

The long-term effect of the Second World War on Boeing was that it allowed the company to assemble a team of experienced work crews and talented engineers in a physical plant of the first magnitude. These factors enabled Boeing during the early years of the cold war to secure defense contracts to build the B-47 and the now-venerable B-52 bombers.

Wartime investments in personnel and material also made possible Boeing's key diversification effort—civilian jet aircraft. The 707, the first successful jet plane to enter commercial service (1958),

The wings of B-17s being prepared for attachment to fuselages.
Courtesy of the Boeing Company.

One of the more visually interesting episodes at wartime Boeing was the attempt to camouflage the plant south of Seattle on the Duwamish River. Up close this rooftop town comes to life. Courtesy of the Boeing Company.

capitalized upon the vacation and business travel that grew with postwar prosperity. A succession of Boeing jets entered this market, most notably the best-selling 727, the 747 jumbo jet, and the latest generation of quieter and more fuel efficient jets, the 757 and 767.

Boeing has not always met with unqualified success. When the federal government scuttled the supersonic transport project, the resulting recession of 1970–71 temporarily crippled Seattle. Both the city and the company recovered, and today the Boeing Commercial Airplane Company remains Washington's largest employer and one of the world's great aircraft manufacturers.

The Boeing Company has never been shy in promoting its geographic roots. Of late, as with the introduction of the 767, Boeing has been fond of posing its new aircraft against the backdrop of the region's spectacular monolith, Mount Rainier. Courtesy of the Boeing Company.

Suburbia

After Pearl Harbor western Washington boomed. The Boeing Company, the Kaiser Shipyards in Vancouver, and the Puget Sound Naval Shipyards hired thousands of workers. Because war workers bought goods from local stores, the Second World War created many new service jobs. It also produced a population explosion. Between 1940 and 1943, Seattle's population increased by more than one hundred thousand.

The resulting housing crisis encouraged a new kind of suburban development. Housing construction had been stalled since before the Great Depression, when most houses were built by small developers who bought lots along a street and created short rows of up to ten or twelve houses. Wartime entrepreneurs established communities on a grand new scale, with tract developments that housed hundreds or even thousands of families. In a flourishing postwar economy, Seattle

Suburban development depended upon transportation, beginning with the streetcars that had extended the city early in the century. After the Second World War, many of Washington's working people went shopping at the automobile dealerships, spending their wartime savings on the cars that enabled them to live in the new suburbs. Courtesy of Special Collections Division, University of Washington Libraries.

Western Washington's suburban growth began during the Second World War, when entrepreneurs built large tract developments to house the many new residents who came to work in the state's war industries. This defense housing was near Tacoma. Courtesy of Special Collections Division, University of Washington Libraries.

had one of the largest proportions of homeowners in the country by 1948.

Many working people used wartime savings to purchase their first cars, and land development continued to follow patterns dictated by the automobile. In Washington those patterns had begun to appear as early as the 1920s. The Pacific Highway, paved through the state by 1924, linked towns throughout western Washington. With the exception of the freeways, the state road system was complete by the Second World War, and by the mid 1950s, Highway 99 linked communities from Everett to Tacoma into a single commercial strip.

Bellevue was settled in 1869, and plans for a steel mill in Kirkland prompted development along the east side of Lake Washington during the 1890s, but these towns remained small as long as they depended on ferries. The Mercer Island floating bridge, which opened in June 1940, facilitated rapid postwar development, although the twenty-five cent toll (with five cents extra per passenger) may have deterred some would-be residents. Bellevue was incorporated in 1953, with a long-range plan designed for automobile traffic.

Four years earlier Bellevue Square had opened, one of the first shopping centers of any kind in the United States. It was soon overshadowed by Northgate, on Seattle's north side. When finished in 1950, Northgate was the first American regional shopping center, defined as one covering more than fifty acres and incorporating a branch department store.

Northgate began as a plan for a single branch of the Bon Marche just north of Lake Union. When it opened in its much less developed location, it featured an outdoor pedestrian mall with a service tunnel running underneath and a four story medical-dental building.

Northgate, shown here decorated for its first Christmas in 1950, was America's first regional shopping center. The parking lot had space for four thousand cars. Courtesy of Special Collections Division, University of Washington Libraries.

World's Fairs

The A-Y-P grounds, shown here in a panoramic bird's-eye view, were located on the University of Washington campus and designed by the famous Olmsted Brothers landscape architecture firm. Courtesy of Special Collections Division, University of Washington Libraries.

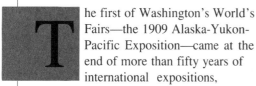

T he first of Washington's World's Fairs—the 1909 Alaska-Yukon-Pacific Exposition—came at the end of more than fifty years of international expositions, beginning with the 1851 Crystal Palace in London. Celebrating human progress and technological ingenuity, the fairs left such permanent landmarks as the Eiffel Tower, built for the Paris exposition of 1889, and such long-lasting legacies from the midways as the Ferris wheel and the ice cream cone.

Seattle's A-Y-P celebration began as a plan to commemorate the Yukon Gold Rush, and expanded into a festival honoring Northwest trade all around what is now called the Pacific Rim. University of Washington history professor Edmond

Much of the construction for Century 21, the 1962 Seattle World's Fair, remained after the event was over, leaving the Seattle Center and the Space Needle as permanent landmarks. Photograph by Forde Photographers courtesy of Museum of History and Industry.

Meany suggested that the fair take place on the university campus, and the famous Olmsted Brothers landscape architecture firm, which was planning parklands all over Seattle at the time, provided a design for developing the 250-acre campus into the fair site. The state appropriated one million dollars, more than one-seventh of its entire budget for the biennium, for the Alaska-Yukon-Pacific Exposition.

The A-Y-P, with exhibits valued at $50 million, opened June 1, 1909, and continued until October 15. The head of the Great Northern Railway, the "Empire Builder" James J. Hill, whom Meany called "the most prominent personality in the economic history of the Northwest," came for the opening. Other celebrities, including President William Howard Taft and industrialist Henry Ford, joined the millions of fairgoers. Although most of the fair was later dismantled, the university acquired several new buildings.

No A-Y-P structure was as prominent as Seattle's own Eiffel Tower, the Space Needle, one of the striking architectural

Century 21 bequeathed two of the modern symbols of Seattle: the monorail and the futuristic Space Needle. Courtesy of Special Collections Division, University of Washington Libraries.

features of the 1962 Century 21 World's Fair. That exposition attracted nearly ten million visitors during the six months it was open. As the civic boosters who promoted it hoped it would, Century 21 brought national attention to Seattle, and despite early problems, it proved to be a financial success.

A dozen years after the Seattle fair, Spokane opened EXPO '74. The city tore down old buildings and cleaned up pollution for this fair, the theme of which was the environment. EXPO's permanent legacy was a park that remains on the site, highlighting the waterfalls so central to Spokane's early development.

Spokane's 1974 World's Fair dramatically changed the heart of the city. Of the tracks and railroad stations removed, only the clock tower of the old Great Northern station remains to remind parkgoers of the waterfront's past. Courtesy of Spokane Public Library.

Indian Fishing Rights

The treaties that Governor Isaac Stevens made with Washington's native peoples in 1854 and 1855 placed Indians on reservations and transferred much of their land to the United States. In the 1854 Treaty of Medicine Creek, signed with the Nisqually and Puyallup peoples, and the 1855 Treaty of Point Elliott, signed with the Muckleshoot, identical language appeared: "The right of taking fish at usual and accustomed grounds and stations is further secured to said Indians in common with all citizens of the Territory . . ." The phrase "in common" proved to be ambiguous enough to provide arguments in court cases throughout the twentieth century.

Controversy began in the mid 1950s when the state sought and received a court order preventing the Puyallup from fishing in the Puyallup River in violation of state conservation practices. Over the next several years, various tribes engaged in

Natural and human victims of "progress" on the Columbia River: the cascades and Indian fishery at Celilo Falls. Courtesy of Bonneville Power Administration.

Exercising treaty rights challenged by the state and by white fishermen, and ultimately upheld by Judge George Boldt and by the United States Supreme Court, these Swinomish Indians were photographed beach seining near La Conner around 1964.
Courtesy of Museum of History and Industry.

public fish-ins, often inviting celebrities to join them, in open violation of state fishing laws.

Probably the most famous of those episodes occurred in 1965 at Frank's Landing on the Nisqually River, when actor Marlon Brando was arrested for net fishing, but released on a technicality and not tried. Ultimately twenty-seven tribes joined to sue in federal court, charging that their treaty rights had been violated.

In 1974 federal Judge George Boldt issued a decision declaring that the treaties did not limit Indian fishing in any way on reservations and guaranteeing Indians half of the salmon caught off reservations. Non-Indian fishermen complained, and the state appealed to the U. S. Circuit Court, where a panel of three judges unanimously upheld Boldt's decision. In the spring of 1979 the United States Supreme Court upheld the decision by a 6-3 vote.

Non-Indian fishing boats block a Washington State ferry in a 1978 protest during the Boldt decision appeals process.
Courtesy of *Seattle Times*.

The 1960s: Protest on the Campus

Washington was deeply divided over the most unpopular military action the United States ever took: the undeclared war in Vietnam and neighboring Southeast Asian countries. Many influential people were deeply committed to supporting the military, which throughout the state's history had contributed much to its economic development. U. S. Senator Henry M. Jackson was one of the most vigorous Congressional supporters of the war.

At the same time, members of a strong antiwar movement campaigned energetically to bring the troops home. Protesters opposed military escalation and violence against demonstrators, and marched in parades welcoming soldiers returning to the United States through Washington's military bases.

The antiwar campaign peaked in the spring of 1970, during several days of protest against the bombing of Cambodia and against the killing of four students by national guardsmen at Kent State University in Ohio and two students by state police at Jackson State College in Mississippi. Ten thousand marchers

In early May 1970, following the American invasion of Cambodia and the killings of student protesters at Jackson State and Kent State, thousands of demonstrators took to the streets in every American city. In Seattle, students marching downtown from the University of Washington took over Interstate 5 in an impressive display of antiwar sentiment. Courtesy of Post-Intelligencer Collection, Museum of History and Industry.

Racial issues were integral to the fabric of protest throughout the 1960s and early 1970s. Here representatives of the Black Panther Party lead a 1969 demonstration at Seattle's Federal Building, calling for the release from prison of the Black Panther leader Huey P. Newton. Courtesy of Post-Intelligencer Collection, Museum of History and Industry.

blocked the Interstate 5 freeway in Seattle for hours, in a march from the University of Washington to the federal courthouse in the downtown area.

Student activism in Seattle, as well as in other parts of Washington, addressed domestic racial issues as well as foreign policy questions. A strong Black Student Union at Seattle Community College joined forces with the Black Panthers and the Students for a Democratic Society to protest the killing of black leaders and de facto segregation in the community college system. Off-campus racial conflict produced acts of violence in Tacoma, Pasco, and Seattle.

The GIs pulled out of Vietnam by Richard Nixon's first troop reduction order landed at McChord Air Force Base in July 1969. Two days later, Seattle streets were full, in a combination military parade, welcome home celebration, and antiwar protest. Courtesy of Post-Intelligencer Collection, Museum of History and Industry.

Mount Saint Helens

Mount Saint Helens was once the loveliest of Cascade peaks. At 8:32 on the morning of May 18, 1980, it stunned Washington and the world when it blasted away its crown with a force five hundred times greater than that of the atomic bomb dropped on Hiroshima in the Second World War. Speeding at two hundred miles per hour, a whirlwind of heat, ash, and debris denuded two hundred square miles of heavily forested land within a fifteen-mile arc to the north. All told the blast killed at least 60 people, an estimated 1,500 elk, 5,000 black-tailed deer, 200 black bears, and literally hundreds of thousands of birds and fish.

A dense, boiling cloud rose from the crater and deposited several inches of ash in eastern Washington and northern Idaho and left its traces even on the East Coast, giving rise to a wry comment: "Don't come to Washington this year; Washington will come to you."

On that Sunday in May and for several days following, the predominant mood in the Pacific Northwest was one of apprehension and fear. Some residents wondered whether this eruption was a prelude to something worse. Perhaps Mount Baker would erupt next. Perhaps the ash was poisonous or radioactive. Yet after cleanup crews reopened streets and highways in eastern Washington, life returned to normal. The Pacific Northwest Regional Commission published a pamphlet called "Exploding the Myth: The Pacific Northwest Remains Beautiful" to counteract any erroneous impressions in other parts of the United States.

In 1983 Mount Saint Helens and its immediate vicinity became a national volcanic monument. Nature is now at work healing scars caused by the eruption.

The serenity of this 1960 scene gives no hint of the explosive power that would detonate twenty years later. Photograph by R.V. Emetaz courtesy of USDA Forest Service.

A plume of ash creates an ominous sky hours after the May 18, 1980, eruption.
Photograph by Jim Hughes courtesy of USDA Forest Service.

Canadian artist Paul Kane painted this dramatic night eruption of Mount Saint Helens during his trip to the Pacific Northwest in 1847.
Courtesy of Royal Ontario Museum, Toronto.

The Politicos: Magnuson, Jackson, Evans, and Foley

U. S. Senators Henry M. Jackson (left) and Warren G. Magnuson (right) had an intimate knowledge of how to get things done on Capitol Hill. Courtesy of Special Collections Division, University of Washington Libraries.

The men and women who represent Washington in the halls of Congress and govern the state in Olympia have been for the most part able people. To be sure, Washington has not been immune to political scandal, corrupt public servants, office-holding nonentities, or political embarrassments. But more than balancing any shortcomings are four prominent names in post–Second World War Washington politics: U. S. Senators Warren G. Magnuson and Henry M. "Scoop" Jackson, U. S. Representative Thomas S. Foley, and governor and later U. S. Senator Daniel J. Evans.

During the years from the mid 1950s until 1980 when the Democrats controlled the Senate, Magnuson and Jackson formed an exceedingly powerful duo, gaining more seniority than any other senators from the North, and more, too, than many of their colleagues from the one-party Democratic South.

Magnuson and Jackson became noted for looking after the interests of Washington. Both were New Deal liberals, but Jackson's support for a strong national defense puzzled other liberals and earned him the reputation of being "hawkish," a derogatory term in the liberal vocabulary. He was accused of being a "Cold Warrior" and the "Senator from Boeing." Even so, he remained unbeatable, serving in Congress from 1941 (in the Senate from 1953) until his sudden death in 1983. In the 1970 election he crushed his Republican opponent with an amazing

U. S. Representative Thomas S. Foley visits with wheat ranchers near Walla Walla.
Courtesy of Representative Thomas S. Foley.

83.9 percent of the vote.

Magnuson served even longer, from 1937 (in the Senate from 1944) until Republican Slade Gorton defeated him in the 1980 election. He held many leadership posts, including the chairmanship of the Senate Commerce Committee.

Congressman Thomas S. Foley is a moderate Democrat who has represented Washington's Fifth District, a stronghold of conservatism that includes both Spokane and Walla Walla, since his election to Congress in 1964. Foley's House colleagues chose him to be Majority Leader in 1987.

When Republicans gained control of the Senate in 1980 for the first time in a quarter of a century, Oregonians Mark Hatfield and Robert Packwood gained powerful positions not unlike those formerly held by Magnuson and Jackson. Joining them after Jackson's death in 1983 was another Republican, Daniel Evans, the only person elected governor of Washington for three consecutive terms and a man rated as one of the nation's ten best governors in the twentieth century.

As governor from 1965 to 1977, Evans proved a popular and able administrator. Trained as a civil engineer, he was well qualified to address the complex issues of administrative reorganization, tax reform, environmental protection, and social justice. As governor, Evans was widely perceived as more liberal than many Democrats. During his term in the Senate, from 1983 to 1988, he surprised some observers by occasionally taking a conservative stance and by deciding in 1987 not to seek re-election to a second full term.

Three-term governor and U. S. Senator Daniel J. Evans.
Courtesy of Senator Daniel J. Evans.

Wet Side/Dry Side

The common impression that Washington is a land of evergreens, ocean mist, and snowcapped peaks contrasts sharply with reality: much of the state east of the Cascades is treeless and semiarid. First-time visitors are often surprised witnesses to the ways mountains and elevation influence rainfall. Most of the world's dry regions result from a planetwide system of air currents, but those of Washington are the product of rain shadows created by mountain ranges.

Mountains influence weather as part of a complex process that begins over the Pacific Ocean. The westerly flow of air across its surface during the winter picks up the moisture later lost over land. Because of the influence of the Pacific Ocean, Seattle and Tacoma experience far less snow and fewer subzero days than the more southerly cities of Saint Paul, Minnesota, and Portland, Maine.

As moist sea air rises to cross the coastal mountains it cools, and like a

Twin pillars of basalt in western Walla Walla County. Situated only a few hundred yards from the Columbia River, the formation is a startling reminder of the semiarid nature of much of eastern Washington. Courtesy of Carlos A. Schwantes.

Early morning clouds of mist shroud the Olympic mountains. Courtesy of National Agricultural Library.

squeezed sponge gives up some of its moisture as rain and snow. The rain coast of the Olympic Peninsula ranks as one of the wettest places on earth. An annual rainfall of 120-140 inches is common and some years can total 180 inches, or the equivalent of two billion gallons of water for each square mile of forest. The result is an evergreen jungle.

Puget Sound receives far less rain and snow. Seattle's annual rainfall is about the same as that of New York City or New Orleans, thirty to fifty inches, but because its precipitation so often falls as drizzle, winter rains may seem interminable and the weather dreary. In Seattle it rains an average of 150 days each year.

When moisture-laden clouds sweep up the face of the Cascade Range they reach higher, cooler elevations than they do in

the Olympic Range. Snowfall on some peaks during the winter months may total three hundred inches and in some years may exceed one thousand inches. Paradise Inn, located at the 5,400-foot level on the south slope of Mount Rainier, recorded a total of 93.5 feet of snow during the winter of 1971–72.

Clouds lose much of their remaining moisture by the time they pass two dozen miles beyond the summit of the Cascades.

Summer in the Palouse country, where winter rains make dry farming possible.
Courtesy of Carlos A. Schwantes.

Farther down the eastern slope the land becomes noticeably drier, and the moisture-loving Douglas firs and ferns that thrive in the dampness of the west side give way to Ponderosa pines and eventually to grasses and sagebrush that survive in areas receiving an average annual rainfall of ten inches or less.

Precipitation gradually increases again as one approaches the Idaho border, from an annual average of six inches along the Columbia River in central Washington to twenty-one inches at Pullman, 140 miles east and 1,300 feet higher.

Wet winters and arid summers characterize Washington, a weather pattern just the reverse of that of the Great Plains. Even on Puget Sound people must water their lawns during the summer to keep them green, and August is a time of forest fire danger.

The camera of Charles Pratsch captured a rare snowfall in Aberdeen in 1903.
Courtesy of Washington State University Library.

History in the Making

Assessing the historical significance of contemporary events is risky business. What seems important today may be just a passing fad, while a phenomenon receiving little attention now could in the long run be of immense significance. Ironically, it is the future that will determine what part of the present constitutes the memorable past.

A few tentative conclusions can still be offered. It would appear that a new Washington economy is emerging to overshadow the state's traditional reliance on extractive industries, notably timber. Washington's beautiful outdoors provides the foundation for a tourism-hospitality industry that may someday surpass the old standbys of logging, agriculture, mining, and fishing as sources of private sector employment.

The state's highly visible tourism promotion program is symbolic of shifting priorities and opportunities. In parts of the state ski resorts, wineries, national parks, volcanic monuments, and modern museums are taking the place of wigwam burners and purse seiners. It is no coincidence that protecting Washington's natural beauty is no longer the concern of the enlightened or sensitive few, but a broad, popular movement that has led to the characterization of the Northwest as "Ecotopia."

Agriculture remains a vital economic activity, yet high technology is a bigger industry than the vaunted apple crop. The health of the computer software industry will have much to do with the future prosperity of Washington. The westward shift of worldwide economic influence, first from Europe to North America and then to East Asia, bodes well for Washington's ports. Will Seattle and Tacoma be to the twenty-first century what Boston and New York were to the nineteenth?

Washington's location on the northeast corner of the Pacific Rim benefited it greatly during the post–Second World War Asian trade boom. In recent years most of Washington's soft white winter wheat has been shipped to Asia where it is made into noodles and other products.

Foreign trade is no new factor in Washington's economic equation. As early as the 1850s, Puget Sound timber was sold in markets all around the Pacific Ocean. In the closing decades of the nineteenth century, Walla Walla wheat was sold on the London market.

Railroad magnate James J. Hill established a steamship company to link

Microsoft of Bellevue and Redmond has become a household "word" around the world because of its computer language and software application programs. The youthful Bill Gates is the mastermind behind the company's success. Courtesy of Microsoft, Bellevue.

*The "Oriental Limited" of the Great
Northern Railway passed Smith Cove when
the steamships* Minnesota *and* Dakota *were
at dock in 1905. The world's largest cargo
carriers at the time, the two ships were part
of James J. Hill's dream of channeling
commerce with the Orient through Seattle
and along his Great Northern Railway.*
Courtesy of Special Collections Division, University
of Washington Libraries.

Seattle with Asian ports. And today
Boeing ranks second in the United States
in terms of its exports, which in the mid
1980s accounted for some 45 percent of
the company's sales.

Perhaps the commercial equivalent of

the Millennium, the Pacific Century, is
about to dawn. Such an event inspired
Thomas Jefferson to commission the
expedition of Lewis and Clark. And
Washington's first governor, Elisha Ferry,
identified the future of the new state with
the same Jeffersonian dream. The
Alaska-Yukon-Pacific Exposition of 1909
represented yet another declaration of
Washington's perceived destiny.

Much of this promise was mere
hyperbole. Ferry's vision collapsed in the
Panic of 1893. The promise of Klondike
gold proved short-lived. And the China
trade, which has captivated American
businessmen for centuries, has yet to
materialize in a meaningful way.

Perhaps when Washingtonians cease

referring to their part of the world as the Pacific Northwest (a continental concept) and substitute for it the term "Northeast Pacific" (an oceanic viewpoint), then we shall know that our destiny has been made manifest.

Vintners are the latest agrarians to utilize the bounty of the Columbia Plateau, creating a number of new wineries. Courtesy of Washington Wine Institute.

In the 1980s, the Port of Tacoma has begun to live up to the promise of a century earlier ("The City of Destiny") and outpaces the Port of Seattle in its movement of cargo. Pictured is the Sea-Land container facility in Tacoma. Courtesy of Port of Tacoma.

"The Evening Gown," 64" by 24" by 24" ceramic sculpture by Marilyn Lysohir-Coates, Bainbridge Island School District. Photograph by Colleen Chartier courtesy of Art in Public Places Program, Washington State Arts Commission.

Contemporary Art

One of the more distinctive features of life in Washington is the vitality of its contemporary art. One clear reason for this is the pace-setting "Art in Public Places Program" of the Washington State Arts Commission.

In effect, a state art collection has resulted from an innovative piece of legislation, passed in 1974, which allocates one-half of one percent from capital appropriations for state buildings for the purchase or commissioning of works of art. The Art in Public Places Program has positioned the finest contemporary art in schools, universities, and other institutions throughout the state of Washington.

This sampler speaks to the richness of a new heritage being created today in this museum without walls.

"Sagebrush Landscape," 30" by 40" oil painting by Cynthia Bennett, Central Washington University. Photograph by Steven Young courtesy of Art In Public Places Program, Washington State Arts Commission.

"Patterned Fawn," 16" by 8" by 15" papier-mâché and bead sculpture by Sherry Marjovitz, Evergreen School District. Photograph by Colleen Chartier courtesy of Art In Public Places Program, Washington State Arts Commission.

Photograph Credits

Photographs in this credit list are given by page number, clockwise from top left corner. The information is presented in this order: page number, archive, negative number.

Archive abbreviations are as follows: American Philosophical Society, Philadelphia, PA: AmPhil; Boeing Commercial Airplane Company, Seattle: Boe; Bonneville Power Administration Archives, Portland, OR: BPA; Chicago Historical Society, Chicago, IL: CHS; Eastern Washington State Historical Society, Spokane: EWSHS; Forest History Society, Durham, NC: FHS; Oregon Province Archives, Gonzaga University, Spokane: GU; Idaho State Historical Society, Boise, ID: IHS; Library of Congress, Washington, D. C.: LC; Minnesota Historical Society, St. Paul, MN: MNHS; Montana Historical Society, Haynes Foundation Collection, Helena, MT: MTHS; Museum of History and Industry, Seattle: MOHAI; National Agricultural Library, Beltsville, MD: NAL; National Archives, Washington, D. C.: NA; National Maritime Museum, San Francisco, CA: NMM; National Park Service, Washington, D. C.: NPS; Oregon Historical Society, Portland, OR: OHS; Port of Tacoma: Port Tac; Public Archives of Canada, Ottawa, Ontario, Canada: Pub Arch Can; Quinault Indian Nation, Taholah, WA: Quin; Royal Ontario Museum, Toronto, Ontario, Canada: ROM; Seattle *Post-Intelligencer:* PI; Seattle *Times:* Times; Sisters of Providence Archives, Seattle: Srs Prov; Smithsonian Institution, Washington, D. C.: Smithsonian; Spokane Public Library, Spokane: SPOLIB; Stark Museum of Art, Orange, TX: Stark; State Historical Society of Wisconsin, Madison, WI: WIHS; The Evergreen State College, Olympia: Evergreen; University of British Columbia, Vancouver, BC: UBC; University of Oregon, Eugene: UO; University of Washington Archives, Seattle: UW Arch; University of Washington, Pacific Northwest Collection, Special Collections Division, Seattle: UW; Washington State Capital Museum, Olympia: State Cap Mus; Washington State Tourism Department, Olympia: Tourism; Washington Wine Institute, Seattle: Wa Wine Inst; Walters Gallery, Baltimore, MD: Walt; Whatcom Museum of History and Art, Bellingham: Whatcom; Washington State Arts Commission: Wa Art; Washington State Historical Society, Tacoma: WSHS; Washington State University, Pullman: WSU; Yale University, Beinecke Library, New Haven, CT: Yale.

Pg. ii: WSHS, Curtis Collection, no #. Pg. iii: Whatcom, Darius Kinsey Collection, 10002 D. Pg. viii: MNHS, 54219. Pg. ix: Tourism, no #; WSU, Pratsch 87-75. Pg. x: NA, no #. Pg. xi: EWSHS, 81-557. Pg. 2: Edward Belcher watercolor, UBC, no #. Pg. 5: UW, no #. Pg. 6: UW, 7596. Pg. 7: WSU, PC-2/78-896. Pg. 8: UW, Harry Humphreys engraving. Pg. 9: ROM, 912.1.72; CR IV-372; WSHS, no #. Pg. 10: Stark, WWc4; cr IV-560. Pg. 11: Stark, WOP7; cr IV-539; WSHS, Edward Curtis, no #. Pg. 12: UW, 7898. Pg. 13: AmPhil, Moulton's Atlas map 126. Pg. 14: Pub Arch Can, Cov. 455, Neg C-41446. Pg. 15: Walt, 290-A. Pg. 16: WSHS, no #. Pg. 18: Smithsonian, no #; NPS, SCBL 151. Pg. 19: OHS, 37563 File 218: OHS, no #. Pg. 20: Yale, no #. Pg. 21: UW, N 979.5 map 24; OHS, 12760 file 1116-1. Pg. 22: UW, N 979.5. Pg. 23: State Cap Mus, no #; UW, N 979.5. Pg. 24: WSHS, no #. Pg. 25: WSHS, Sohon drawing; WSHS, no #. Pg. 26: Smithsonian, 45,744; WSHS, no #. Pg. 27: WSHS, no #. Pg. 28: Srs Prov, no #; GU, no #. Pg. 30: UW, N 979.5 map 71; WSHS, no #. Pg. 31: UW, N 979.5 map 55; UW, N 979.5 map 62. Pg. 32: UW, 4370. Pg. 33: State Cap Mus, no #; Whatcom, Kinsey, 10002. Pg. 34: Richard Piper, no #. Pg. 36: MTHS, Haynes Foundation Collection, H-996. Pg. 37: MTHS, Haynes Foundation Collection, H-2631; WSU, 81-059. Pg. 38: UW, no # ; Tom Stilz, no

#. Pg. 39: WSU, no #; MOHAI, 1755. Pg. 40: UW, Kinsey 1542; MOHAI, Picket 15327. Pg. 41: UW, 7570; UW, Lee 1117. Pg. 42: MTHS, Haynes Foundation Collection, H-999; MTHS, Haynes Foundation Collection, H-3313. Pg. 43: MNHS, HE10 page 280 1465; MOHAI, 1604. Pg. 44: UW, 1675. Pg. 45: MOHAI, 16056; OHS, 13182. Pg. 46: WSU, 78-783; WSHS, Curtis 48572. Pg. 47: NMM, I11.27522n.; MOHAI, 2700. Pg. 48: NMM, Hester Collection, F20.17,887nl. Pg. 49: NMM, F9.12,432.nl; NMM, F5.25,387.nl; NMM, U60.12,435.nl. Pg. 50: UW, no #. Pg. 51: WSU, 87-001; WSU, 78-125; WSU, 78-982. Pg. 52: OHS, 11436; Whatcom, Kinsey Collection, 10076 D. Pg. 53: UW, Kinsey 1765; UW, Kinsey 3683. Pg. 54: LC, LC 4779; UW, Postcard Collection. Pg. 55: MOHAI, 1124; WSU, 78-102. Pg. 56: WSHS, LOGLU 65. Pg. 57: WSHS, LOGLU 63; WSHS, LOGLU, 67. Pg. 58: UW, I&O 146. Pg. 59: UW, I&O 138 (Curtis 63844); LC, LC 4731. Pg. 60: LC, McCormick Collection, LC 4731; MOHAI, 10593. Pg. 61: LC, McCormick Collection, LC 4731. Pg. 62: WSHS, Curtis 22058. Pg. 63: WSHS, Curtis 1058; MTHS, Haynes Foundation Collection, H-1161. Pg. 64: MOHAI, 1153. Pg. 65: MOHAI, 8354; MOHAI, 13053; MOHAI, 17886. Pg. 66: WSU, 79-055; UW, I&O Curtis 14713. Pg. 67: UW, 7574; MOHAI, 12819; UW, Kinsey 492. Pg. 68: EWSHS, L84-327.2094. Pg. 69: MOHAI, 11510; UW, I&O Cobb 3801; UW, I&O Curtis and Miller 27682. Pg. 70: MOHAI, 4636-064; WSHS, Asahel Curtis photograph. Pg. 71: MNHS, 54215; WSHS, Asahel Curtis photograph. Pg. 72: EWSHS, Latham 4807; WSHS, Morse 465. Pg. 73: EWSHS, J. Peltier Collection, 184-327, 831C; Quinault, *Portrait of Our Land* page 11. Pg. 74: WSHS, no #; EWSHS, F-98. Pg. 75: LC, US Geographic File 1478; UW, 2318; MTHS, Haynes Foundation Collection, H-2047. Pg. 76: MNHS, GN HE2791.G7. Pg. 77: UW, 7577; WSU, no #; OHS, no #. Pg. 78: UW, Fire Collection 1889, #29 Neg 409. Pg. 79: UW, Fire Collection 1889, #35 Neg 2192; EWSHS, no #; UW, 5435. Pg. 80: State Cap Mus, no #. Pg. 81: CHS, no #. Pg. 82: State Cap Mus, no #. Pg. 83: State Cap Mus, 14; State Cap Mus, 13. Pg. 84: LC, LC 1768. Pg. 85: MOHAI, 83.10.6400. Pg. 86: WIHS, 39942. Pg. 87: LC, LC 1768-968; LC, LC 1768-967. Pg. 88: MOHAI, 1091, slide 4000. Pg. 89: WSHS, 26368; WSHS, Curtis 26440. Pg. 90: WSHS, Pamphlet Collection 979.755, Su74. Pg. 91: EWSHS, LA9 P.42; UW, Postcard Collection. Pg. 92: UW, Curtis 19943. Pg. 93: UW Arch, Nellie Fick papers, box 1; UW Arch, Joseph Smith papers, box 10-6. Pg. 94: WSHS, Pamphlet Collection 979.755, Su74. Pg. 95: OHS, Pamphlet Collection; MNHS, GN HE2791.G7. Pg. 96: UW, 7537; IHS, no #. Pg. 97: UW, 6633. Pg. 98: UW Arch, Ault Collection. Pg. 99: UW, 2274; WSHS, Curtis 21766. Pg. 100: EWSHS, 6472. Pg. 101: LC, US Geographic File, Washington State; OHS, 31644 #1092. Pg. 102: WSU, 78-124; OHS, no #. Pg. 103: LC, US Geographic File, Washington State; OHS, 77236, File 997; UW, Curtis 28875. Pg. 104: UW, Monte Cristo 2041. Pg. 105: UW, 2097; UW, Curtis 23588. Pg. 106: UW, Curtis 1885. Pg. 107: UW, Hoquiam File; WSHS, no #; UW, Lee 2373. Pg. 108: LC, US Geographic File, Washington State, Seattle. Pg. 109: UW, Farquharson Collection, # 12. Pg. 110: UW, Lee 20022. Pg. 111: EWSHS, L85-105.8; UW, 4812. Pg. 112: WSU, PC-2, Box 3. Pg. 113: UW, I&O Curtis 15085; WSHS, Pamphlet Collection 979.788 L867. Pg. 114: MOHAI, 15693. Pg. 115: UW, Curtis 25305; WSHS, Mss. Stubbs Box 2 File Church Programs. Pg. 116: UW, 2055. Pg. 117: UW, 14580. Pg. 118: WSHS, no #. Pg. 119: LC, US Geographic File, Washington State, Tacoma; UW, 7567. Pg. 120: UW, 7572; UW, 7576. Pg. 121: MOHAI, 83.10.7025; WSU, 78-866.

Pg. 122: MOHAI, 11934. Pg. 123: UW, 7512. Pg. 124: UW, Waite 198-10. Pg. 125: UW, 8238; UW, Seattle theaters 871. Pg. 126: UW, Curtis 65146. Pg. 128: UW, no #. Pg. 129: WSHS, no #. Pg. 130: WSU, 78-342; MOHAI, 7164. Pg. 131: BPA, no #. Pg. 132: UW, Kinsey 1912; Eduardo Calderon, no #. Pg. 133: NAL, 282777; WSHS, Pam 979.788 L867. Pg. 134: UW, 1530. Pg. 135: UW, Port Townsend 5086; UW, Postcard Collection 7571. Pg. 136: MOHAI, 1994. Pg. 137: NAL, no #; EWSHS, no #. Pg. 138: NA, 86-g11 F-7; MOHAI, 6338B. Pg. 139: WSHS, Curtis 38414. Pg. 140: MOHAI, 69379 W&S. Pg. 141: MOHAI, 69378 W&S; UW, Documents #2 Neg 4085. Pg. 142: MNHS, 54220. Pg. 143: MOHAI, 9661; UW, I&O 5793; EWSHS, L86- 327.1396. Pg. 144: WSHS, Pamphlet Collection, 979.731 Sp65t; LC, US Geographic File, Washington State, Olympic National Forest. Pg. 145: UW, 7569; UW, 7573. Pg. 146: WSHS, Curtis 24552. Pg. 147: UW, 7578; UW, Curtis 40152. Pg. 148: LC, US Geographic File, Washington State—Bays, Lakes, and Rivers; WSHS, Curtis 31258. Pg. 149: MOHAI Sports 648. Pg. 150: UW, Lee 21011; Lee 20102. Pg. 151: WSHS, Ginther Collection #63; UW, no #. Pg. 152: MOHAI, 15,540. Pg. 153: WSHS, Curtis 32873. Pg. 154: WSHS, Pamphlet 979.7371. Pg. 155: UW, Pamphlet Collection Snoqualmie Falls. Pg. 156: LC, LC SS Files, Dams—Washington, Grand Coulee LC-USZ62-91300. Pg. 157: EWSHS, 392; UW, 232. Pg. 158: UW, 1661. Pg. 159: NA, 52- 3134, 306 PS; EWSHS, L85-143.120. Pg. 160: UW, 6354. Pg. 161: MOHAI, PI-22102; NA, 56-13685; UW, no #. Pg. 162: OHS, 49684. Pg. 163; MOHAI, 989; FHS, no #. Pg. 164: MOHAI, PI-28084. Pg. 165: MOHAI, PI-28050; NA, RG 210-G Box # 19. Pg. 166: NA, PS306, 49-5642. Pg. 167: WSHS, Pamphlet Collection 979.751 R399ri; NA, PS306, B 56-9818. Pg. 168: Boe, P4065. Pg. 169: Boe, P5143; Boe, no #. Pg. 170: UW, World War II neg 734; UW, 7575. Pg. 171: UW, 6044. Pg. 172: UW, AYP neg 1378; MOHAI, Century 21 #2673/32. Pg. 173: UW, 856; SPOLIB, no #. Pg. 174: BPA, no #. Pg. 175: MOHAI, 9913; Times, *Where the Mountains Meet the Sea*, by James R. Warren. Pg. 176: MOHAI, Post-Intelligencer Collection, Thomas photograph #2A/3. Pg. 177: MOHAI, Post-Intelligencer Collection, Barlet photograph #25A; MOHAI, Post-Intelligencer Collection, Barlet photograph #23/23A. Pg. 178: R. V. Emetaz photograph USDA For Svc, no #. Pg. 179: Jim Hughes photograph USDA For Svc, no #; ROM, no #. Pg. 180: UW, no #. Pg. 181: Rep. Thomas S. Foley, no #; Sen. Daniel J. Evans, no #. Pg. 182: Carlos Schwantes, no #; NAL, 519955. Pg. 183: Carlos Schwantes, no #; WSU, Pratsch #57. Pg. 184: Microsoft, no #. Pg. 185: UW, 6577. Pg. 186: Port Tac, no #; Wa Wine Inst, no #. Pg. 187: Wa Art, Colleen Chartier photograph; Wa Art, Colleen Chartier photograph; Wa Art, Steven Young photograph. Pg. 190: Tourism, Tom Stilz photograph, no #. Pg. 196: MTHS, Haynes Foundation Collection, H-2079.

The Columbia River Gorge formed the Northwest's most important natural highway through the Cascades. Courtesy of Washington State Tourism Division.

Index

Daisy, 159
Dayton, 87
de Hezeta, Bruno, 12
Democratic Party, 40–41, 80–81, 130, 180–181
Denny, Arthur, 120
Denny, David, 148
Depression. *See* Great Depression
DeVoe, Emma Smith, 92–93
Disque, Colonel Brice P., 139
Douglas County, 86, 158
Duniway, Abigail Scott, 92
DuPont, 112–113

Education: colleges and universities, 120–121; community
    colleges, 121; elementary and secondary, 118–119
Electric interurban railroads. *See* Railroads
Electricity: hydroelectric power, 46, 152–155, 159
Ellensburg, 78, 82
Engineering, civil, 108–111
Ephrata, 160, 163
Equality Colony, 99
Ethnic groups, 61, 70–71, 74, 123; English, 70, 71; Finns, 70, 71;
    Germans, 74, 137; Greeks, 61; Hispanics, 70, 132; Italians, 70,
    71; Norwegians, 38, 70; Scandinavians, 38, 61, 70; Slavs, 61;
    Swedes, 38, 70, 71. *See also* Asians
Evans, Senator Daniel J., 180, 181
Evans, Elwood, 76
Everest, Wesley, 141
Everett, ix, x, 75, 103, 106
Everett Massacre, 96, 97
EXPO '74. *See* Fairs and expositions

Fairchild Air Force Base, 135
Fairhaven, 86
Fairs and expositions, 144; Alaska-Yukon-Pacific Exposition,
    172–173, 185; Century 21 (Seattle), 172, 173; EXPO '74
    (Spokane), 100, 173
Farley, James, 99
Ferry boats, 39, 106
Ferry County, 86
Ferry, Governor Elisha P., 80, 185
Fidalgo, Salvador, 12
Finns. *See* Ethnic groups
Firdale, 115
First World War, 136–139; and Boeing, 168; economic effects
    of, 128–129, 134, 136–137; and military, 134; and
    radicalism, 96, 129, 139, 140–141; and shipbuilding, 64–65,
    128, 136
Fisheries, Department of, 61
Fishing and canning: early history, 58; technology, 59–61, 69
Flagg, Ernest, 82

Foley, Congressman Thomas S., 180, 181
Ford, Henry, 173
Forts: Canby, 134; Casey, 134; Colville, 15; Flagler, 134; George
    Wright, 134; Lawton, 130, 134; Lewis, x, 134, 135, 163; Nez
    Perce, 7; Nisqually, 15; Okanogan, 15, 22; Vancouver, 7,
    14–15, 16, 20, 28; Victoria, 15; Walla Walla, 7, 15, 134;
    Ward, 134; Worden, 134, 135
Franklin, 45
Franklin County, 86, 132
Frederick and Nelson Department Store (Seattle), 104
Freeland, 99
Fremont, Jessie Benton, 21
Fremont, John C., 21
Friday Harbor, ix
Fur trade, 4, 6, 14–15; Hudson's Bay Company, 6–7, 10, 14–15,
    22, 24, 47; North West Company of Montreal, 14; Pacific Fur
    Company; 14

Garfield County, 86
Gates, Bill, 184
Gibbs, George, 16, 19
Glover, James, 75
Gold mining. *See* Mining, gold
Gonzaga University, 121
Gorton, Senator Slade, 181
Goss, F. H., 83
Grand Coulee, 158
Grand Coulee Dam, viii, 151, 154–155, 156–159, 160
Grange. *See* Washington State Grange
Grant County, 50, 86, 132, 158
Gray, Captain Robert, 12
Grays Harbor, 61, 64, 70
Grays Harbor County, 85
Great Depression, 129–130, 150–151, 158, 170
Great Northern Railway, 53, 173; development activities, 44, 75;
    and immigration, 70; promotional activities, 34, 88, 95, 144
Greeks. *See* Ethnic groups
Green Lake, 100
Guthrie, Woody, 157

Hanford, 162, 166
Hanford Project, 155, 162, 166–167
Hanson, Mayor Ole (Seattle), 140
Hester, Wilhelm, 48
Highways. *See* Roads and highways
Hill, James J., 44, 54, 75, 173, 184–185
Hirabayashi, Gordon, 164
Hispanics. *See* Ethnic groups
Home, 99
Hoquiam, 65
Hudson's Bay Company. *See* Fur trade
Hutton, May Arkwright, 93
Hydroelectric power. *See* Electricity

Idaho Territory, 31
Inchelium, 159
Industrial Workers of the World (IWW). *See* Radicalism
Island County, 84

Jackson, Senator Henry M., 176, 180–181
Jefferson, President Thomas, 13, 185
Jefferson County, 84, 85

Kaiser, Henry J., 162
Kaiser Shipyards, 162, 170
Kamiakin, 25
Kane, Paul, 10–11
Kelley, Hall Jackson, 16
Kettle Falls, 159
King County, ix, 70, 84
Kinsey, Darius, 33
Kirkland, 112, 171
Kitsap County, 85
Kittitas County, 70, 86
Klickitat County, 85
Klondike Gold Rush, 39, 88–89, 172

Labor: agricultural, 50–51, 66–67, 91; child, 123; coal mining, 62–63; ethnic groups, 60, 61; fishing, 60–61, 69; gender, 61, 68–69, 137; industrial violence, 63, 97; logging, 52–55, 139; publications, 96, 123; shingle weaving, 56–57, 97; shipbuilding, 64–65, 136; unemployment, 150–151; union activity, 96–97, 129, 139, 140–141; wageworkers' frontier, 66–67; World War One, 136–137, 139. *See also* Radicalism
La Conner, 125
Lake Chelan, 147
Lake Washington, 39, 108–109, 127, 149
Lake Washington Ship Canal, 108–109
Lander, Edward, 120
Landes, Bertha, 128
Lewis and Clark Expedition, x, 6, 13, 185
Lewis County, x, 84
Liberty Lake, xi, 145
Lincoln County, 1, 86, 158
Long, R. A., 113
Long Lake Dam, 153
Longmire, James, 144
Longview (Monticello), 113
Loyal Legion of Loggers and Lumbermen, 139
Lumber industry, 132; early history of, ix, 52–55; forest fires, 54; sawmills, 56; shingle weaving, 56–57; Spruce Production Division, 137, 139; stump farming, 55; technology, 52, 53, 55, 56–57

Mackenzie, Alexander, 13
Magnuson, Senator Warren G., 180, 181
Malaspina, Alejandro, 12
Manhattan Project, 153, 166
Mapping the Pacific Northwest, 13, 21, 22
Marcus, 159
Mason City, 158
Mason County, 85
McChord Air Force Base, 135, 163, 177
McClellan, George, 22
McLoughlin, Dr. John, 7, 14–15
Mead, Governor Albert, 82–83
Meany, Edmond, 118, 124, 173
Meeker, Ezra, 76
Mercer, Asa Shinn, 76
Mercer, Thomas, 108
Mercer Island, 127
Microsoft, 132, 184
Military, 134–135, 136–139, 162–163; Corps of Topographical Engineers, 22; United States Air Force, 135, 163; United States Army, 16, 20, 21, 22, 27, 134, 135, 139, 163; United States Army Corps of Engineers, 108, 109, 154; United States Navy, 20–21, 64, 103, 134, 135, 162. *See also* Forts, individual installations
Miller, Alfred Jacob, 15
Mining, coal, 62–63, 66, 70; gold, 68, 88–89
Missionary activity, 7–8, 16, 28; Catholic Ladder, 19; Catholic missions, 28; Father Joseph Joset, 28; Mother Joseph of the Sacred Heart, 28; Protestant missions, 16; Protestant Ladder, 19; Saint Paul's Mission, 28; Sisters of Providence, 28; Society of Jesus, 28; Spalding, Rev. H. H. and Eliza, 19; Father Urban Grassi, 28; Waiilatpu, 18, 21; Marcus and Narcissa Whitman, 7–8, 16, 21, 24, 28, 116
Monroe Street Bridge, 111
Moses Lake, 163
Mount Baker, 23
Mount Index, 34
Mount Olympus National Monument, 146
Mount Rainier, 12, 144, 169, 183
Mount Rainier National Park, 146
Mount Saint Helens, x, 178–179
Mount Saint Helens National Volcanic Monument, 178
Mukilteo, 58
Mullan, John, 22
Murrow floating bridge, Lacey V., 127

Native Americans: Bannock, 20; Cayuse, 16, 27; Chinook, 3; Coast cultural area, 4–5, 6, 11; Colville, 159; Crow, 36; Dawes Severalty Act, 73; fishing rights, 9, 24, 159, 174–175; fur trade, 4, 8, 14; impact of disease on, 6; land holdings, 73; Makah, 5; Muckleshoot, 174; Nez Perce, 9, 24, 26, 72; Nisqually, 24, 174; Nootka, 4; place-names from languages, x, 85–86; Plateau cultural area, 4, 5–6, 11, 24, 27, 72; Puyallup, 24, 174; Quinault, 73; reservation era, 72–73, 174; Salish,

S

San Juan County, 85

Sawmills. *See* Lumber industry

Seattle: Denny Regrade, 110; economic activity, 162; fairs, 172–173; fire of 1889, 78–79; General Strike, 129, 140–141; Health Department, 137; and Klondike, 39, 88–89; and military, 163; Municipal Railway, 106; parks, 114, 130, 148–149; population characteristics, ix, 38–39, 68, 74, 75, 100–101, 152; Port of, 102, 186; and radicalism, 96, 97, 98, 99, 137; and railroads, 44, 45, 46, 106; and shipbuilding, 64, 136; and shipping, 48, 62; Street Railway, 106; and student activism, 176–177; and suffrage, 92–93; University of Washington, 100, 120; urban development, 100–102, 106, 127, 152; weather, 182

Seattle Community College, 177

Seattle University, 121

Second World War, 131, 162–165; atomic bomb, 166; and Boeing, 168; economic effects of, 154, 162, 170; Japanese American relocation, 164–165; and military, 162–163; and shipbuilding, 64, 131

Shipbuilding, 64–65, 136, 162

Ships: sailing, 48–49; steam, 47

Sisters of Providence, 28

Skagit County, x, 86

Skamania County, 85

Skinner and Eddy, 64

Skykomish, 40

Smith, Levi Lathrop, 32, 74

Smith Building, L. C., 101–102

Snake River, 47, 111

Snohomish County, 85

Snoqualmie Falls, 155

Snoqualmie Pass, x

Soap Lake, 163

Sohon, Private Gustavus, 27

Sol Duc Hot Springs, 144

Spalding, Rev. H. H. and Eliza. *See* Missionary activity

Spanish explorers, 12

Spanish influenza, 137–138

Spokane: as county seat, 87; EXPO '74, 173; fire of 1889, 78, 104; Free Speech fight, 97; Monroe Street Bridge, 111; National Apple Show, 90; population characteristics, 39, 68, 75, 100; as proposed capital, 29; and radicalism, 96–97; and railroads, 46, 106, 107; urban development, 75, 100, 102, 152

Spokane County, x, 70, 85, 87

Spokane River, 100, 152

Spokane War, 27

Spokan Garry, Chief, 27

Spruce Production Division, 137, 139

Stadium High School (Tacoma), 119

Stanley, John Mix, 6, 11, 22, 23

State Equal Suffrage Association, 93

Steamboats, 47

Stevens, Governor Isaac I., 9, 22–23, 24–27, 76–77, 174

Stevens County, 85

Stores and shopping, 104–105, 170

Strait of Juan de Fuca, x, 58

Streets. *See* Roads and highways

Strong, Anna Louise, 137, 140

Student movements, 1960s, 176—177

Stump farming, 55

Suburbia. *See* Urbanization

Sunnyside Project, 94–95

Swan, James G., 76

T

Tacoma: economic activity, 38, 64; and military, 163; population characteristics, ix, 39, 100; Port of, 186; as proposed capital, 82; and radicalism, 96; and railroads, 43, 44, 46, 77, 106; and shipbuilding, 64; and shipping, 48, 62; urban development, 100, 102, 152; weather, 182

Tacoma Land Company Hotel, 119

Tacoma Narrows Bridge, 109, 111

Tacoma Seamen's Friend Society, 114, 115

Taft, President William Howard, 173

Terry, Charles, 120

Theatre Comique, 124

The Dalles, 6, 24

The Evergreen State College, 121

Third Avenue Theatre, 106, 125

Thomson, R. H., 110

Thurston County, 82, 84

Tieton, 95

Titus, Dr. Hermon F., 98

Tono, 113

Tourism, 144–145, 184

Truman, President Harry S, 166

Tumwater (New Market), 32

U

United States Air Force. *See* Military

United States Army. *See* Military

United States Navy. *See* Military

University of Washington, 43, 120, 137, 143, 172–173, 176–177

Urbanization, 74–75, 78, 100–103, 114–115, 127, 170–171; company towns, 112–113

V

Vancouver, Captain George, 12–13

Vancouver: population characteristics, 131; as proposed capital, 82; and shipbuilding, 64, 131, 162

Vancouver Barracks, 134

Vancouver Shipyard, 162

Vanport Flood, 155

Varney Air Lines, 130

Vietnam War, 176–177

Villard, Henry, 42

W

Wahkiakum County, 85

Y

An 1890 view up the falls that made Spokane a pioneer in the development of hydroelectric power.
Courtesy of Haynes Foundation Collection, Montana State Historical Society.

The Editors

General Editor **Carlos Schwantes** is an accomplished amateur photographer and a widely recognized expert in Pacific Northwest history. He is a professor of history at the University of Idaho and author of numerous books and articles about the Pacific Northwest. A specialist in labor history, Schwantes most recently completed a general work called *The Pacific Northwest: An Interpretive History* (University of Nebraska Press, 1989). He received his Ph.D. degree in history from the University of Michigan in 1976.

Contributing Editor **Katherine Morrissey** is an assistant professor of history at Williams College in Massachusetts. A social and cultural historian, she has studied the creation of communities in the Pacific Northwest, with special attention to the creation of the "Inland Empire" centered on Spokane. Morrissey, who will receive her Ph.D. degree in American Studies from Yale University in 1988, combines a thorough understanding of the historical development of the American West with a discerning eye for meaningful images.

Contributing Editor **David Nicandri** is director of the Washington State Historical Society in Tacoma, having previously served as curator of history at the Washington State Capital Museum in Olympia. For the past fifteen years he has been an active leader in state and local historic preservation organizations, serving as the founding president of the Washington Trust for Historic Preservation and founding secretary of the Washington Museum Association. He earned a M.A. degree in history at the University of Idaho in 1972.

Contributing Editor **Susan Strasser** is the author of the prize-winning book *Never Done: A History of American Housework* (Pantheon Books, 1982). Her expertise in researching and interpreting visual evidence is a major element in her scholarly achievement and has contributed significantly to the quality of *Washington.* She received her Ph.D. degree in history from the State University of New York at Stony Brook in 1977.

Washington: Images of a State's Heritage
Design and consulting services, Laing Communications Inc., Bellevue, Washington.
Art direction, Sandra J. Harner—Production assistance, Candice Duncan Cross.
Set in 10 point Times Roman with captions in 10 point Times Roman Italic and credit lines in 8 point Times Roman.
Printed on 80 pound acid-free Dynawhite Cougar Opaque Smooth.
Paper provided courtesy of the Fine Paper Division, Weyerhaeuser Paper Company.
Color separations, printing, and binding by Publishers Press, Inc., Salt Lake City, Utah.
Typesetting by Spokane Imagesetting, Spokane, Washington.
Published by Melior Publications, Spokane, Washington, 1988.